ROOMS OF OUR OWN

ROOMS

of our

own

SUSAN GUBAR

UNIVERSITY OF
ILLINOIS PRESS
Urbana & Chicago

Library of Congress

Cataloging-in-Publication Data

Gubar, Susan, 1944–

Rooms of our own / Susan Gubar.

p. cm.

Includes bibliographical references.

ISBN-13: 978-0-252-03140-3 (cloth : alk. paper)

ISBN-10: 0-252-03140-7 (cloth : alk. paper)

ISBN-13: 978-0-252-07379-3 (pbk. : alk. paper)

ISBN-10: 0-252-07379-7 (pbk. : alk. paper)

1. Feminist theory. 2. Feminism. 3. Sex role.

4. Women—Social conditions—21st century.

I. Title.

HQ1190.G82   2006

305.4201—dc22   2006003048

OCLC 63472612

What we need today more than ever is a feminism
committed to seeking justice and equality for
women, in the most ordinary sense of the word.
Only such a feminism will be able adequately
to grasp the complexity of women's concrete,
everyday concerns.

—TORIL MOI, *What Is a Woman?*

Who beside myself could give me the authority
to speak for us?

—STANLEY CAVELL, *A Pitch of Philosophy*

Sing me
something (the sound of the low wave-breaking)
(the tuning-down where it deposits life-matter on
the uphill of shore)(also the multiplicity
of deepenings and covering where whiteness rises as a
manyness)
(as the wave breaks over its own breaking)
(to rip in unison)(onto its backslide)—
of something sing, and singing, disagree.

—JORIE GRAHAM, "Evolution," *Never: Poems*

CONTENTS

CHAPTER 1

THE ONCE AND FUTURE HISTORY
OF SEX AND GENDER

FROM WHERE I stood, by the banks of a little stream on the
edge of a great expanse of lawn in one of those public institutions of higher education that have sprung up all around the
globe, half-dressed young men and women could be seen lolling under trees budding with newly unfurled leaves. Frisbees
were tossed back and forth by the sleepers' vertical counterparts, and the far-off beat of a boombox (was it hip-hop or
techno-trance?) could barely be detected, buffeted by the sweet
spring breezes. Once, not very long ago, this prospect with its
walkways and massive buildings was prairie too, where corn
and wheat waved or swine rooted and cattle grazed. Teams of
workers must have hauled the stone in trucks from the neighboring quarries, and then the huge beige blocks were hoisted
up to be placed one on top of another, and then the plumb-
ers brought their pipes, and the glaziers their glass, and the
roofers their shingles. Marking the end of the ragged lawn and
turning the green into a quadrangle, half a dozen structures
stood in a hodgepodge of styles. One rising eight stories high

out of limestone, quite a few smaller buildings limestone too, with tendrils of ivy curling around ersatz Gothic windows, still others plain concrete or squat in red brick or refurbished private houses: the college depended upon public funds, and over the years various committees of trustees and administrators, hampered by insufficient budgets, clearly had to choose the cheapest bids from local construction companies. Though the campus had its beauties—wooded areas and gardened plots, a world-class manuscript library, a state-of-the-art theater and musical arts center—neither the gold of kings and presidents nor the silver of parliamentarians and legislators had poured liberally into the foundations of these plain, serviceable classrooms and offices, some in evident need of renovation. The term "architecture" hardly seemed to apply.

Still, it was a sunny, fresh scene, with the sky washed of clouds and shedding warmth from its blue, with purple and yellow crocuses clumped amid the tree roots and moss beside the brook. Foam frothing over the little stones and larger rocks in the streambed, which put me in mind of chemical spills, prevented me from taking off my shoes and socks to dip my toes in the fast-flowing water, but not from letting down the line of my thoughts, really just a string of associations. A barely perceptible tug—an idea at the end of my rod—pulled me upright, as a tumult of ideas about the transformation of women's situation in the twenty-first century flashed through my mind. A baby fish, not much weightier than a minnow, swam to and fro in my thoughts. It had something to do with what feminists began quite a few decades ago: the disentangling of gender from sex, of social roles from biological genitalia, of masculinity from males and femininity from females. I start here, with this reverie beside the stream that wanders through the campus where I teach, because I attribute to it the origins of my series of meditations on women's once and future history. But, you might say, what does women's once and future history have to do with the quadrangle I now surveyed? I suspect, though, you would admit that competing definitions of sex and gender abound within such buildings as these. Biologists, with all their talk of XX and XY chromosomes or testosterone and estrogen, disagree with psychologists, with their analysis of identifications with mom or dad; post-structuralists, who trade in what they call performativity, quarrel with anthropologists, sociologists, and law professors, who tout race, region, religion, class, age, and sexual orientation. This is because they, in turn, have been influenced by historians and literary critics trained in postcolonialism, cultural studies, or queer theory. If, however, you are either a newcomer to these debates or a person with dimming memories of bygone school days, you might exclaim, What are the premises of geneticists, post-structuralists, or queer theorists; who (besides academics) should care about them; and have their conversations altered the situation of women or the evolution of feminism?

Likewise, if, and perhaps especially if, you have spent a good share of your conscious life bearing in mind women and their well-being, you may be as intensely absorbed as I am by the questions, What advances have women made and what still needs to be done? Should you pursue your life's work inside or outside the academy, it must be obvious that all these queries have been debated intensely within colleges and universities, where their answers have also been made manifest. A consideration of the impact of feminism on higher education and of higher education on feminism might require an investigation into the campus life of women teachers and their students; or it might focus on feminist intellectuals and the methodologies they have developed in their various scholarly disciplines; or it might tackle women's studies and the programs it has pioneered; or it might mean that somehow all these are inextricably mixed together with arguments about sex and gender. It was when I had begun thinking about the subject in this last way that my head ached and a drowsy numbness swept over me, so I had paused by what I could hardly call a river, wondering first (I admit) if it was polluted and then, as the title of this book floated toward the surface of my mind, what its four monosyllabic words should elicit.

Were I to begin at the beginning, my comments might range from a few remarks on Aristotle's view of the female as an insufficient man to more recent arguments that the broken Y makes man a genetically incomplete woman. They could examine how great artists like Aeschylus and Cervantes, Shakespeare and Goethe, Marcel Proust and Toni Morrison envision the relationship between men and women, or what such theorists as Engels and Levi Strauss had to say about the aetiology of sexual arrangements. Drawing on the *Oxford English Dictionary*'s definitions of gender (stemming from *genus*, "race," "kind," from the root "to produce"), my chapters might rehearse the history of feminist speculation from Christine de Pizan and Mary Astell to Kate Millett and Germaine Greer about the creature Simone de Beauvoir defined as a member of "the second sex." When I began to consider the interconnections among all these possibilities, though, I soon realized how bored and boring I would be undertaking such a hopeless, hapless task because so much ink has been spilled on many of these subjects, but also because I would never be able to get to the present day. And it was the confusion of the present day (if—thinking like historians—we consider that phrase to mean the last three or four decades) that fascinated me. For (and here I quickly try to offer you that nugget of truth authors of short books pride themselves on) sex and gender became especially contested terms during the period when an appreciable number of women finally began to earn the money that enabled them to rent or own, furnish, and decorate rooms of their own, when the women's revolution effected remarkable and long-reaching changes in people's lives, when feminism made a definitive mark on higher education and higher education made a definitive mark on feminism. While Virginia Woolf—speaking only nine years after women gained the vote and entrance into a few of the professions in England—emphasized the mystic potential they might bring into being, we have witnessed startling transformations that have not only released many middle-class women from the constraints of traditional gender roles but have also complicated the idea of gender itself. Why this is and what it means continue to baffle me so I have determined to show you how I came to hold the view that the many definitions of gender and sex abounding at the turn of this century have generated a multiplication of feminisms (decidedly in the plural), variegated political forms and intellectual forums not all coherent or congruent, some downright contradictory, but nonetheless exhilarating and empowering for the female of the human species. No longer singular anomalies or eccentric tokens in the production of culture, women today have not fully attained the status of insiders either; what

that curious situation means about women, about feminism:
this is the substance of the rest of these pages.

Some eighty years ago, the muse of my undertaking passionately believed that since it is impossible to tell the truth
about highly controversial subjects, one has a responsibility to
explain how certain beliefs came to take hold and to explain
in such a manner that readers could draw their own conclu-
sions as they observe the prejudices of the writer. I will therefore make use of the license of novelists, letting lies prolifer-
ate so as to tell a fictitious story about one year of events which
shaped my belief that especially those women with sufficient
money and rooms of their own face bewildering but unprec-
edented prospects today.

There I was, then, a few years ago, but now sounding and
looking even less the way I really do (call me Mary Beton, Mary
Seton, Mary Carmichael, or any name you please), leaning
against the railing of a narrow brick-lined wooden bridge, the
gift of a graduating class from the sixties. Unfortunately, given
what may strike you as evasions or then again my heated pro-
pounding of proposals later qualified or dismissed, you might
feel some exasperation about blunders that repeatedly bungle
my apprehension. Indeed, irritation not only at my gaffes and
biases but also at my zigzags of mind may cause you to want to
hurl these pages in the recycling bin, where they might serve a
clear purpose. For, mine (you will see) is a character-in-prog-
ress, and over the passage of time, I rarely end up concluding
what I started out believing. Since I am confessing my qualms
here at the beginning, this may be the place to concede, in other words, that you may find me somewhat bewildered or befuddled, often in need of instruction from my colleagues and

friends. It is, of course, for you to decide whether any part of these meanderings is worth keeping; yet, lest I seem to protest too much, I should admit to harboring a hope that my telling the past by installments may afford you a crash course in feminist intellectual history.

Albeit cursory, even cartoonish at times, my descriptions of women teachers and students, feminist intellectuals and methodologies, women's and gender studies programs are meant to encourage you to compare our situation at the beginning of the twenty-first century with what our predecessors faced in the early twentieth century, which is why I invite you to return to that moment by the stream when I exulted that the uncoupling of gender from sex had changed the relationships between many middle-class men and women and could eventually rearrange them for many others to achieve more equitable societal arrangements. But before I could recite the mantra "sex is to gender as nature is to culture," the carillon chimed. It was time, I realized, to make my way to the class I was supposed to attend that afternoon, so I scrambled up and walked rapidly toward the high-rise.

Instantly, just as I neared the entrance, two figures intercepted me, though initially I hardly understood the meanings of their gesticulations. Only when I was close enough to hear their spiel did it become clear that the first sought to offer me a "free gift" (a coffee cup) in exchange for my filling out a credit card application, while the second was thrusting a Bible at me, presumably for the salvation of my benighted soul. They had sent my little minnow into hiding, which was probably for the best since I realized now that I was almost late. In fact, the course called Women and Fiction that I was supposed

to observe would begin in a matter of minutes and so I rushed
toward the elevators, hoping that not all of them were out of
commission. Back in the days when I was an undergraduate,
such classes in women's literature didn't exist, I mused, trying
to turn my mind away from my minnow (lost amid the hawkers
with their material and spiritual goods) and instead toward the
group of undergraduates I would encounter under the aegis of
a newly appointed part-time instructor, one Marita Seton.

Questions persisted, though. Why was the campus filled
with credit-card hucksters, I couldn't help wondering. Most
of the students had to work off campus to supplement their
loans and their scholarships, their parents' contributions,
and their savings from summer jobs. As for the Bible salesman—no that wasn't fair, I admonished myself—as for the
missionary on the grounds, I had seen him for years, even
knew his name (Max), had to admit grudgingly his devotion
to his cause since he preached rain or shine, during the hu-
midity-drenched summer session as well as the freezing winter quarter. Much more eloquent an orator than the homeless
stutterer we used to call "The Yumkie Man" at the frightfully
dangerous and filthy subway entrance adjacent to the elite urban college I had myself attended some thirty years ago, since
all he said was "Yumkie! Yumkie!" (or was it "Yankee!" or
"Yummy!" or perhaps "Your key!") . . . but at this point I became exasperated with the pointlessness of my musing and its
jumble of senseless associations.

Again, in an effort to concentrate on the work at hand (why
Marita had asked me to observe her), I checked to see if I had
sufficient blank pages in the pad in my tote, for this bright and
ambitious young woman would be attempting the job market

once again next fall, looking for a permanent, full-time position, and in need of a letter of recommendation from me tes-
tifying to her teaching excellence. One lone elevator seemed to
be working, and I waited for its arrival with a growing group of
undergraduates amassing next to a bulletin board affixed with
notices about yoga classes, child-care facilities, a production of
Carmen, and lessons in Yiddish, sign language, jazz guitar, and
feng shui. Reminding myself to avoid the bruises knapsackers
unwittingly inflict in close quarters and expecting someone
would key the third floor, I rode the elevator noting how many
undergraduates these days look like humpbacked mountain-
eers or back-woods campers, even in their scanty spring garb.

My watch said 1:10 and it was time to find my way down the
corridor to what turned out to be a littered classroom holding some twenty-five students pretzeled into those chairs
with arms that widen out into desktops. Arranged in a semicircle, they faced a woman who looked young enough to be
my daughter, although I was not sure I would want any offspring of mine sporting a crew cut (giving off a vague sheen
of chartreuse), a pierced nose (a stud? a jewel? happily not a
ring!), a see-through paisley blouse (but surely there was an
undershirt beneath the filmy material?), and a short skirt that
looked like it had been made by stitching together two silk
scarves, one for the front, the other for the back. On her feet,
pointy high-heels made me anxious about her balance. Still,
Marita's charm was her dark eyes (were they Chinese or Spanish?), oblique in her coppery face.

It is a curious fact that novelists have a way of making us
believe that college classes are memorable for something very
witty or wise that is said, but they seldom mention what cloth-

ing was worn and with what effect, no less what food was consumed in these environs. That the students did not seem in
any way disconcerted by the net effect of Marita Seton's appearance may have been related to their own blatant eccen-
tricities in haberdashery. As with the alpine trekkers in the
elevator, many of those undergraduates not displaying flip-
flops wore alarmingly high-tech sneakers on their feet and
denim or khaki jeans (cut off at various lengths and angles)
for trousers. On the young women, these were topped off with
tiny velvet-, satin-, or lace-trimmed tanks that must have
shrunk in the wash. Whereas the slim as well as the plump
girls looked a bit constricted (their hips, midriffs, and belly-
buttons in plain view), the young men swam in T-shirts many
sizes too large and baseball caps worn backward (the flap apparently better suited as neck-guard than visor).

Despite my professorial uniform (a dark pantsuit with a
turtleneck beneath the jacket), I could recall my own forays in
bygone days—first tight black sweaters and jeans, then colorful peasant blouses, followed by mini skirts—but still, I felt,
the fashions had never been quite so strange: everyone had
marketing logos printed everywhere, advertisements for various brand names, or artful designs, mystic symbols in red and
blue tattoos peeping out on pelvises or shoulders, thighs or
ankles. Odder still (or was this an effort to sustain the moun-
tain-climbing motif?), most held water bottles, plastic containers with nipple-like stoppers at which they perpetually or
periodically sucked. All but one—an unkempt, earnest young
man grunting with satisfaction over his notebook—had a Xeroxed handout (presumably "Fantomina," the assignment for
the day) open to display its yellow highlighting. Alpine to the

extreme, he (the grunter) had arranged a row of jelly beans on his notebook next to a wristwatch, as if to time his steady intake of the candy (which, to my amusement, is exactly how he spent his fifty minutes in the class). On the board appeared the following list of characters:

1. Fantomina
2. Celia
3. Widow Bloomer
4. Incognita

These names brought to mind the plot of this narrative gem by Eliza Haywood, an early eighteenth-century novelist, essayist, and pamphleteer. The characters on the blackboard were the various personages Haywood's heroine plays in the course of a rather remarkable short story.

Intrigued at the theater by the sight of men openly flirting with prostitutes—I had reread the assignment myself the night before in preparation for the class—a rich, unnamed lady becomes curious and decides to deck herself out as the whore Fantomina. Imagine her surprise when the accomplished Beauplaisir courts her in a manner deeply gratifying because so unrestrained. Desirous of seeing him again, she manages to obtain a secret lodging where his visits eventuate first in a quasi-seduction, quasi-rape ("she was undone; and he gained a victory") and then in the sustained bliss of a highly satisfactory affair maintained without Beauplaisir's ever discerning her real identity. So far, so good, I had thought the evening before. By teaching a work composed before the twenty-first century and a short story so obviously about the passion of a woman dedicated to pursuing her own desire, Marita could

subvert the complacency of students about their own libera-
tion from the lesser lives of people not lucky enough to dwell
amidst the postmodernity of microwaves, microchips, and
the pharmaceutical alleviation of PMS.

The fly in the ointment of Haywood's tale, though, is the
fickle male of the species. Beauplaisir was a philanderer or a
rake: "he varied not so much from his sex as to be able to prolong desire to any great length after possession: the rifled
charms"—a nice phrase worth repeating!—"the rifled charms
of *Fantomina* soon lost their potency, and grew tasteless and
insipid." Yet the crafty and wealthy heroine immediately forms
a stratagem; she disguises herself as a maid, gets herself hired
by the landlord with whom Beauplaisir is staying, and enjoys
being ravished as the prettily naive Celia. When Beauplaisir
grows weary of Celia, she in turn metamorphoses into the sor-
rowful Widow Bloomer; and when he gets bored with Widow
Bloomer, she then takes on the character of the mysteriously
aristocratic Incognita, whose sexual generosity fans his flames,
though her imperious decision not to show her face threatens
to douse them. In effect, Fantomina tricks herself out in a succession of tantalizing female figures whom Beauplaisir can enjoy thinking he has seduced and abandoned.

How sad that a rather abrupt deus ex machina closes Haywood's spicy story: the arrival, first, of Fantomina's formidably
strict mother and, then, of a fetus whose growth can be camouflaged by tight lacing and hoop-petticoats but whose determination to be born cannot be denied during a grand ball at court.
Haywood's heroine "could not conceal the sudden rack which
all at once invaded her; or had her tongue been mute, her wildly
rolling eyes, the distortion of her features, and the convulsions

which shook her whole frame, in spite of her, would have revealed she labored under some terrible shock of nature." Poor Fantomina finds herself packed off with her baby to a French monastery ruled by an abbess who is a particular friend of her mother.

On my right in the back of the room, POP went an orange jelly bean, followed by a grunt of satisfaction, as Marita called the class to order, explained the publishing history of "Fantomina," and asked the students to consider why Haywood's heroine begins and sustains her series of masquerades.

"She's guarding her reputation," piped an animated girl with a nimbus of fierce golden curls and bright purple lipstick. "Doesn't want to be labeled a slut."

"She's a croquette, curious about sex," muttered an Asian boy, shaking his dredlocks. "Ladies aren't supposed to know about sex so she wants to find out what prostitutes know. She rocks my socks; what she's got is 'wild and incoherent' desires!"

As I noted on my pad how dexterous Marita was at sparking discussion, they all agreed that Fantomina might think she was setting out to gratify "an innocent curiosity," but really she wanted to discover what men were like when they were not kept in a state of reserve by her high station and reputed virtue.

"Isn't she at the theater when she first puts on the act?" The black young woman who had called this out wore a retro-fifties outfit: Peter Pan collar on a white cotton blouse, gold circle pin, pleated plaid skirt.

"Yes, Nell!" exclaimed Marita. "She's a kind of artist, in other words, like a stage actress. What were you going to say, Arthur?"

A slight boy in (of all things) a suit paused before intoning his words slowly and distinctly. "What none of you realize is she stands in for Haywood. It is obvious to me that Fantomina is the artist within the text, engaged in setting scenes, creating plots and dialogue, a surrogate for Haywood."

POP, grunt: a yellow bean gone.

"Puh-*lease*, but, like, doesn't she have to be?" Nimbus of curls interjected. "First, she can't get real action from the Beau-guy because he sort of worships the ground of ladies like her and then, like, after he makes it with her as a whore, he gets bored right away and wants—like, you know—different types."

Next to a cluster of quiet note-takers, the girl sitting beside me (was her Walkman switched off?) had used a pen to etch the letters A I D S on the broken arm of her desk and was now boxing it in with a series of horizontal and vertical gashes in the already splintered wood. Each of her fingernails was painted a different color.

On the board, Marita had written under "Fantomina" the words "constancy of desire" and "multiplicity of roles"; under "Beauplaisir," "inconstancy of desire" and "stable identity."

"What about the specific parts Fantomina decides to take on?" Marita asked. "Are they significant? A prostitute, a maid, a widow, Incognita."

"How can you write 'stable identity' next to the Beau?" asked Dredlocks.

Someone on my right (whom I couldn't see) responded. "Well, she's got lots of names; he's only got one."

"Yeah, if, like, being a rapist is a 'stable identity,' I guess he's got one," Nimbus agreed. "He's into the ravishing thing, see, like, he 'glutted each rapacious sense with the sweet beauties of the pretty *Celia.*'"

"Excellent use of the text!" Marita beamed. "Aren't all the characters Fantomina plays vulnerable in uniquely female ways?"

"None of you get it," Arthur the Suited intoned; "I mean, the whore, the maid, and the widow symbolize the economic and social secondariness of women in the eighteenth century. Obviously, these female characters reflect the alterity of women in Haywood's time. I use the term 'alterity' to gesture toward Beauvoir."

"*Whatever*," groaned Nimbus, shooting Dredlocks a look of anguish, while on my pad I put down the word "self-restraint" to remind myself how Marita kept her face mildly attentive to Mr. Avuncular.

POP went a red bean and the sleeve of the Peter Pan blouse rose up.

"How come Beauplaisir keeps on getting fooled? Is he some kind of idiot, or what?"

"Good question, Nell," Marita nodded. "Anyone have an answer?"

"Take a look at the bottom of page 215," Nimbus said and then quoted: "'she was so admirably skilled in the art of feigning, that she had the power of putting on almost what face she pleased, and knew so exactly how to form her behavior to the character she represented, that all the comedians at both playhouses are infinitely short of her performances: she could vary her very glances, tune her voice to accents the most different imaginable from those in which she spoke when she appeared herself.'" She took a long swig of water with evident relish.

"Plus he deserves what he gets," Dredlocks agreed. "He's unfaithful to Fantomina, Celia, the Widow, and the Cogito; he lies to them all about how much he adores them. He's a polygamist—that's his Achilles tendon. He's trying to get into their pants so she manipulates him back."

Marita paused for a second, while I sneaked a look at the now baroquely boxed A I D S (was it a call for help or a comment on the anachronism of Haywood's plot?) and the impassive face of my neighbor (who looked thin, though healthy, but who can tell).

"Does Haywood actually propose Fantomina's scheme as a solution to the problem of male inconstancy and sexual rapacity?" Marita asked.

"Fantomina can play the whore or the maid, but they can't play her," Nell murmured to herself, barely loud enough to be heard through the voice-over of the authoritative Arthur.

"That would be a good question, if it had not already been so blatantly answered by the text itself," Arthur sniffed, puffing up to quote from his copy of the story. "'O that all neglected wives, and fond abandoned nymphs would take this method!— Men would be caught in their own snare, and have no cause to scorn our easy, weeping, wailing sex!' Obviously, Haywood as an artist is proposing Fantomina's feminine wiles as a crafty response to philandering men. Anyone can see that. What's more interesting is how unreliable the narrator is. I sense a distance between the author and the narrator that would undercut the entire discursive regime so that Haywood's relationship to the narrator reflects the narrator's to Fantomina, and Fantomina's to Celia and the Widow—which makes the whole text a metafiction. Note the incursion of the epistolary form!" He flushed.

The eyes of Dredlocks and Nimbus rolled back in their heads so only the whites showed, but Marita didn't see this because she had been fumbling around, trying to switch on an overhead projector. Unable to do so, she read aloud two quotes she later wrote on the board.

1. "Reflect on the whole history of women: do they not *have* to be first of all and above all else actresses. . . . They 'put on something' even when they take off everything. Woman is so artistic." —Nietzsche

2. "What do I mean by masquerade? In particular, what Freud calls 'femininity.' The belief, for example, that it is necessary to *become* a woman, a 'normal' one at that, whereas a man is a man from the outset. He has only to effect his being-a-man, whereas a woman has to become a normal woman, that is, has to enter into the *masquerade of femininity*." —Irigaray

"I'd like you to take out a sheet of paper," Marita instructed the class, "put your name on it, and spend the next ten or so minutes writing about the issues raised by Nietzsche and Irigaray; that is, the relationship between femininity and impersonation or performance. Certainly this seems to be the point of 'Fantomina' as well as our discussion about it." The girl next to me fumbled with her Walkman, pocketed her pen, got up, and left the room. How difficult it is to know what is going on inside our students, I fretted; their private ills, their personal problems with family and friends, their raging hormones, the buzzing in heads that makes it so very hard for them to hear, and learning itself—to which Marita and I had dedicated ourselves—how well nigh impossible it sometimes remains for many.

Grunts punctuated POPs while everyone else scribbled in their notebooks, each sustained (in Herculean struggles with Continental philosophy) by periodic nursing on their water bottles. Contending with the gloom threatening to dampen my spirits, I thought, what a clever way for Marita to bring up the idea of female socialization. How many *male* members of the faculty had a mirror in their office desk drawers—to check their "rifled charms"? "Fantomina," Marita had taught me, could be read as a comment on Nietzsche's and Irigaray's ideas about the masquerade of femininity, on how women are taught to watch themselves being watched, survey themselves being surveyed by men. After all, the only power available to Haywood's heroine consists in her ability to impersonate those feminine roles Beauplaisir will find intriguing and attractive. The chalk letters on the blackboard—"what Freud calls 'femininity'"—blurred as I squinted at "a man is a man from the outset," for what was desirable about dad, not mom, was the real power in the world the male organ has historically symbolized. Although Fantomina creates the erotic spectacles that so titillate the libertine looking for a succession of conquests, although she thereby controls the man who would seduce and abandon her, she must confine her imaginative scenarios to what will whet his capricious appetites.

For both of Haywood's characters, eroticism remains a matter of power politics: conquest of women (for him) and retention of the male (for her). In the *folie à deux* (it's called codependence these days) between titillated hunter and titillating prey, did the rake and the coquette deserve each other? Perhaps this might explain the significance of the final guise (the inscrutable Incognita) and Beauplaisir's revulsion against not being allowed to see the face of the woman so generously bestowing her body upon him, so adamant about not showing her features:

He said all that man could do, to prevail on her to unfold
the mystery; but all his adjurations were fruitless; and he
went out of the house determined never to re-enter it, till
she should pay the price of his company with the discov-
ery of her face and circumstances.

The masked face of Incognita and even the names "Incognita" and "Fantomina" might be said to symbolize how little we
know about the true nature of womanhood. "Nothing so true
as what you once let fall," Haywood's nemesis Alexander Pope
once wrote; "*Most Women have no Characters at all.*" For centuries women have performed a phantasmagoric pantomime for
men and maybe still do (what else could rising rates of anorex-
ia, rising ratings of Madonna and Janet Jackson mean?).

But there was one major difference between Fantomina and,
say, Nimbus and Nell or, for that matter, Madonna. *Griswold v.
Connecticut* (1965), *Roe v. Wade* (1973); birth control, choice—
with those rights, Fantomina might have enjoyed a long life of
adventurous sexual escapades, might have circumvented "the
sudden rack," "the convulsions" shaking her whole frame, the
"terrible shock of nature." Even if Fantomina forgot to use birth
control last month, she could have access to a morning-after pill
or to an abortion. Perhaps instead of assigning fluidity to social
roles, we should consider the malleability of biology. Could it be
possible that it has been and will be easier to adapt nature than
to alter nurture, easier to change the body than the mind?

Marita, collecting the students' papers, noted the intense
gaze of the grunter, whose desk—now barren of beans—contained not even the show of written work, though he was a bit
older than the rest, a returning student (and they are usually
the most serious about their labors).

"Yes, Harry?" she smiled, her (Chinese? Spanish?) eyes dancing.

"What I don't get is this: since Fantomina knows Beauplaisir is a liar—grasping, groping, but then totally turned off, always on alert for another skirt—why does she still keep wanting him? I mean, hasn't she got better things to do with her time?"

Ah, I saw with rising elation and all of a sudden, this, *this exactly* is what had changed since Haywood's time, and *this* is what remains marvelous about teaching. Who would have expected the unkempt and seemingly unprepared jelly-grunter would be the one to come up with it? Had the other students heard (they were packing their knapsacks, collecting their bottles), comprehended its import? Today Fantomina is free to desire all kinds of things: a position on the Supreme Court or the job of prime minister, a trip down the Nile or a cottage on Cape Cod, first chair in the cello section of the Chicago Symphony Orchestra or a residency in a Bangladesh teaching hospital, a freelance business in graphic design or training in oceanography, law enforcement, computer programming. Hard work and determination and sacrifice—with a dash of luck and talent—might or might not make these goals possible; however, Beauplaisir was no longer a necessary ticket to happiness or success. For a lady like Fantomina, whose destiny revolved around becoming a wife and a mother, the only conceivable form of empowerment involved the erotic manipulation of men (or a hard fall into the demeaning stature of whore, maid, widow, eccentric). If contemporary women need not produce the phantoms of a femininity mimed when a sexual division of labor ruled the economies of most of the world, a colossal shift in the relation-

ship between the sexes had certainly occurred. Humming "I'm
Just Wild About Harry," I signaled to Marita (who was closing
the class with the promise of further discussion) my intention
to meet her later (she taught back-to-back literature courses so
she could commute to a community college to pick up composition classes at night) to discuss what the English department
would call my "peer visitation" and then hurried up a staircase
at the end of the hall to the floor above.

Closing the door of my office, I perused the books on my
shelves and pondered Haywood's resonant tale. How odd the
contrast between the inventive fluidity of Fantomina's variously adopted guises to attract and hold on to Beauplaisir, on
the one hand, and, on the other, the stark biological doom that
seals her fate when she finds her whole frame wracked by labor convulsions. This juxtaposition between social roles and
the "terrible shock of nature": what did it dramatize if not the
great divide between gender and sex? Whore or maid, widow
or mysterious lady, Fantomina displays the fictitiousness, the
multiplicity, the mutability of gender, of the engendering of
femininity itself. Donning different clothes and expressions,
she cons a series of quite divergent economic, social, and
erotic identities quite distinct from her biological makeup.
Haywood's uncanny insight into the gulf between social gender roles and physiological sex was far from unusual. Centuries before the word "gender" itself came into prominent use,
feminists had struggled to disentangle the unstable mobility of
culture from the fixity of nature.

Here is Mary Wollstonecraft, for example, I thought, taking down her *Vindication of the Rights of Woman.* Her courage
and uncompromising idealism—she had lain as a child on the

landing to prevent her father from beating her mother—were
bolstered by the revolt against tyranny she witnessed during
the French Revolution. One has only to open her 1792 book,
a treatise extending the liberty of fraternity to the equality of
sorority, to find her railing against the issue of nature. Although "the female in point of strength is, in general, inferior
to the male," she admits, men—refusing to be "content with
this natural pre-eminence"—"endeavour to sink us still lower,
merely *to render* us alluring objects"; "women, in particular,
are *rendered* weak, and wretched" by a "false system of education" instilled by men who consider females "rather as women
than human creatures." When a girl child is "*rendered* dependent" by overprotection, Wollstonecraft asserts, "dependence
is called natural." As in the rendering of fat, the rendering of
female human creatures into feminine creations means re-
ducing, converting, or melting them down. So debilitating
is feminization for Wollstonecraft that she believed "the few
extraordinary women" who resolved to rush "in eccentrical
directions out of the orbit prescribed to their sex, were *male*
spirits, confined by mistake in female frames"; in other words,
women who managed to evade the engendering of femininity
were virtually transsexuals.

Because she suffered terribly from melancholy that sometimes led to suicidal depression, Wollstonecraft composed
out of bitterness that transmutes into cheerier tones in her
American successor Margaret Fuller. I turned over the pages
of Fuller's "The Great Lawsuit" and seemed to hear the naiveté
and hopefulness of the New World championing the spiritual
equality of a resurrected womanhood after all arbitrary barriers were torn down:

We would have every path laid open to women as freely as
to man. Were this done, and a slight temporary fermenta-
tion allowed to subside, we believe that the Divine would
ascend into nature to a height unknown in the history
of past ages, and nature, thus instructed, would regulate
the spheres not only so as to avoid collision, but to bring
forth a ravishing harmony.

As if buoyed by faith in an American egalitarianism that would
spread to establish an Edenic garden of gender equality, a vision of exuberant redemption unfurls and expands in Fuller's
phrases. I reflected on Fuller's understanding that "there exists in the minds of men a tone of feeling toward women as toward slaves" and, after a pause in which I pushed some junk
mail back into the overflowing wastepaper basket, on her determination to lead women out of bondage. Capacious and elas-
tic, Fuller's belief in nature's hybridity grounds her optimism.
Since "it is no more the order of nature that it should be in-
carnated pure in any form," it makes sense that "male and female represent the two sides of the great radical dualism. But,
in fact, they are perpetually passing into one another. . . . There
is no wholly masculine man, no purely feminine woman." Not
hermaphroditic but androgynous, human nature also profits
from nature's love of exceptions, leading Fuller to predict the
imminent birth of a "female Newton" and a "male Syren."
    What harasses Wollstonecraft, what inspires Fuller is ex-
actly what would perplex John Stuart Mill a few decades later,
specifically how little we know about nature, how often we label "natural" whatever behavior (no matter how debilitating)
seems conventional or conditioned and thereby set it in stone,
deem it "innate" or "hardwired":

So true is it that unnatural generally means only un-customary, and that everything which is usual appears natural. The subjection of women to men being a univer-sal custom, any departure from it quite naturally appears unnatural. But how entirely, even in this case, the feeling is dependent on custom, appears by ample experience.

Whether or not he was only recording the original thoughts of his brilliant intimate Harriet Taylor (and he did call her "the inspirer" as well as "in part the author" of "all that is best in my writings"), Mill keeps on asserting that "it cannot now be known how much of the existing mental differences between men and women is natural, and how much artificial; whether there are any natural differences at all; or, supposing all artifi-cial causes or differences to be withdrawn, what natural char-acter would be revealed." In other words, the pretty blushes and modest deference of the maid Celia are no less learned by the actress Fantomina than by her real-life counterparts, the prettily blushing, modestly deferential maids of Haywood's day or, for that matter, our own. And so, I considered, the charwoman stationed within an inn in a sixteenth-century Ba-varian village, the house slave within an antebellum plantation in Mississippi, and the maid within the Hong Kong Holiday Inn at the turn of the twentieth century would obviously dis-play their skills as well as their charms (and their resentment at having to manifest them) in registers as diverse as their lan-guages and costumes would necessarily be.

Why, then, did Wollstonecraft and Mill and their succes-sors have to come back over and over to this effort to denatu-ralize gender, to distinguish it from biological sex? And was it still necessary to pursue what seemed on the surface such a bla-

tantly reasonable, even undeniable insight? Olive Schreiner—
writing during the dawn heralded by the breakdown of rigid
Victorian sexual ideologies (with their separate public spheres
for men, private spheres for women)—returned to hammer the
point home repeatedly in passionate but interminably thwart-
ed and disappointed outbursts about unjust relations between
the sexes. Tormented by feminine socialization (and by her
own absorbing self-pity), Schreiner's New Womanly heroine
Lyndall decries the crippling effects of "rendering" human
beings into women:

> It is not what is done to us, but what is made of us . . . that
> wrongs us. . . . We all enter the world little plastic beings,
> with so much natural force, perhaps, but for the rest—
> blank; and the world tells us what we are to be, and shapes
> us by the ends it sets before us. To you it says—*Work!* And
> to us it says—*Seem!*
>
> We fit our sphere as a Chinese woman's foot fits her shoe,
> exactly, as though God had made both—and yet he knows
> nothing of either. In some of us the shaping to our end
> has been quite completed. The parts we are not to use
> have been quite atrophied and have even dropped off; but
> in others, and we are not less to be pitied, they have been
> weakened and left. We wear the bandages, but our limbs
> have not grown to them; we know that we are compressed,
> and chafe against them.
>
> Do you think if Napoleon had been born a woman that he
> would have been contented to give small tea-parties and
> talk small scandal? He would have risen; but the world
> would not have heard of him as it hears of him now—a
> man, great and kingly, with all his sins; he would have left

one of those names that stain the leaf of every history—the
names of women, who, having power, but being denied
the right to exercise it openly, rule in the dark, covertly,
and by stealth, through the men whose passions they feed
on, and by whom they climb.

Surely, as these torrents of roiling prose demonstrate, the earnest young revolutionary of *The Story of an African Farm* has been
distracted and disabled by a wounding engendering that crush-
es the human soul, inculcates in women precisely those du-
plicitous arts Fantomina exploited, atrophies the female body,
and produces dependent, manipulative creatures whose need
to feed off men made Schreiner call them "female parasites."

After putting Schreiner back on the shelf and quickly
checking for the signs of either "rifled charms" or "parasitism"
in the mirror inside my desk drawer (though nothing could
be done with the limp page-boy—had the henna streaked orange?—and a dusting of blusher failed to brighten washed-out
cheeks), it seemed appropriate to leap to the novelist who so
lyrically depicted the material and psychological impediments
to the full flowering of women's creativity and to the philoso-
pher who made famous the idea that "one is not born a woman,
but rather becomes one." For with Virginia Woolf and Simone
de Beauvoir we turn an important crossroad on the map of
feminist protest and analysis. We leave behind the great souls
desperately gathering names for petitions, organizing meetings, networking at lectures so as to try to persuade recalcitrant
societies to give women political, educational, economic, and
social rights. We come to the time right after the First and then
the Second World War when at least some advantaged women
in a few Western countries could vote, hold office, attain law or

medical degrees, inherit stocks or land, obtain divorces and even the custodial rights over their own children. And hadn't Woolf and Beauvoir understood fascism as an ideology of sexual difference that inscribed as natural and eternal law the warrior hero and the prolific mother? But a knock on the door put an end to my reading. Marita, standing in the hall, waited to accompany me down the staircase (the previously working elevator was stuck between floors—with passengers who kept pressing the screaming alarm) and through paths on which innumerable undergraduates explained into cell phones (to friends? to parents?) that they, too, were making their way at the present moment over to the Student Union, where a perfectly dreadful food court had replaced a perfectly dreadful cafeteria.

There was the line for Burger King, there the queue for Pizza Hut, there the one for SubConnection; a new sign for "Sushi— Fully Cooked!" filled me with trepidation. Individual portions in carton containers sat sweating on aluminum shelves under heat ducts, alongside an odd assortment of (also individually packaged) yogurt, cereal, muffins, chips, pretzels, trail mix, power bars, and juice boxes. In a transient space crowded with round plastic tables arranged on white-and-orange checkered linoleum, a setting that resembled an intersection in an airplane terminal or a mall, Marita and I allowed ourselves the luxury of fantasizing about the amenities of a faculty club (there should have been upholstered armchairs arranged on Persian carpets, little glasses of sherry and Camembert with grapes and crackers, mahogany end tables with emerald-green reading lamps) before her latte and my cappuccino soothed our frayed nerves. In a few minutes we were sipping from our steaming

Styrofoam and slipping freely amid all those objects of curiosity that form in the mind after a shared experience and that are
naturally to be discussed on coming together again: how stuffy
was the suited Arthur, how unexpectedly smart the bean-eater;
had the Walkman girl gotten sick? And wasn't it extraordinary
that Eliza Haywood so many centuries ago anticipated recent
feminist insights? All these were sprinkled with compliments
on Marita's teaching that might embolden her to attempt the
terrible job market again.

For I had delegated myself Marita's unofficial mentor and
wanted to do what I could to facilitate her professional success
during a period of time (it had lasted longer than most expected) when multiple retirements occurred every spring, whereas
replacement hiring was postponed or curtailed every fall. As I
worried, though, that she would never get one of the few advertised tenure-track assistant professorships if she wore a see-
through blouse (without underwear?) to an interview, she was
trying to overcome her concern about the absence of an auditor named Chloe, who was not the sort to cut, being one of the
brightest in the class. So Marita fretted—there were rumors of
an obnoxious boyfriend and a week's worth of absences—while
I pondered the tact of mentoring, where my responsibility had
to be circumscribed by what she might feel to be hurtful or ma-
tronizing meddling.

While these things were being said and thought, however,
I became aware of a melancholy drift setting in of its own accord and threatening to carry me as well as our conversation
forward. The doubling up of part-time teachers, the polluted
brook and greasy cartons, the stalled elevators and broken
projector, the proliferating litter, the credit-card and Bible

peddlers (I am giving you my thoughts as they came to me): this hodgepodge of images had me at its mercy, so I found myself wondering if women had entered higher education at just that moment when higher education was deteriorating in all too many manifest ways. Did vocations and professions get devalued because women began to participate in them, or were women allowed to do them only when they were in the process of becoming depreciated? Rather than subject Marita to a conversation that would further demoralize her about a situation over which neither of us had any control, I firmly banished the Persian carpets, upholstered armchairs, emerald-green reading lamps, and even (regretfully) the sherry, for that comfortable and congenial faculty club had been exclusively inhabited by a highly elite class of men made crabby and encrusted by their exclusive traditions. Back then, too, Nimbus and Nell, Dredlocks and most especially I'm-just-wild-about-Harry would never have been allowed entrance into the college classes they so resplendently grace today. So, repeating a phrase to myself, "the amenities would have to wait," I resolutely turned back to Marita's class on "Fantomina."

"Don't women still put on a masquerade of femininity today?" I asked Marita, mentioning Madonna and *Mademoiselle*, *Ally McBeal* and the Indigo Girls to display my (albeit scanty) store of popular culture bits.

"Not Madonna, it's Britney Spears's body parts, Ani DiFranco, and 'reality' TV shows—they're all the rage. But the coquette and the rake are figures flagrantly out-of-date now, as out of date as Ally McBeal!" Marita assured me that chastity was no more valued in young women today than sexual rapacity was in young men. "Judging from the advertisements during those evening game shows—for free six-pack samples of Viagra—the number-one sexual problem today is hardly the one Fantomina faced!"

"Shame on you, Marita," I laughed, noticing with relief that there was an undershirt beneath the filmy blouse, though unable to ascertain if the skirt was really made of scarves. "But if chastity was so important in Haywood's time, so trivial now, it must be hard to teach her."

"What makes it hard to teach," Marita sighed, "is my students' thinking I'm just some sort of wannabe-babe who has to be monitored by a 'real' professor. Not to mention their hostility to anything that smacks of feminism, though maybe poor Haywood is partly to blame." She quickly continued with a laugh. "Even Virginia Woolf thought 'she was a writer of no importance,' that 'no one reads her for pleasure.' She's very funny about how the names of Haywood's 'romances make us droop'; 'the mazes of her plots' make us 'swoon away.'"

"Poor Fantomina," I sighed in agreement (since I didn't know Woolf had written about Haywood, but then on what woman writer hadn't she ruminated, and of course I realized that Marita might have felt anxious about being observed). "Imagine her being confined after her confinement in the convent by her puritanical mother. Your excellent class, it made me wonder, which was—is—more important: nurture or nature, gender or sex, education or birth control."

"But," Marita objected, "the convents of France were run by terrifically enterprising women. Why, Fantomina had a whole new stage for her charades and with a female audience at her disposal. A great place to bring up her daughter!" I thought she hadn't heard all that I had said until she continued. "My mother went to a convent school because it was a tradition for the women in her family, and she had a pretty racy youth. But her grandmother had eight children and my mom only had two, and that was *after* she got her pilot's license and the job with the airline that provided the best parents' compensation package." She stirred what was left of her drink and added, mostly to herself, "I might not have any at all."

I could almost see Marita's great-grandmother in my mind's eye, a Chinese or Spanish lady wrapped in a plaid shawl, surrounded by her hordes of children, their laundry, their coughs and earaches, their insistent demands that she watch their dazzling performances on bicycles, skates, and swings. How could she possibly have found time to amass a fortune or acquire a profession, to become the aviator she dreamed of being, the pilot her granddaughter would become? Even her daughter (the mother of Marita's mother), born in the momentous year of 1919, could only fleetingly imagine exchanging her mother's hand-me-down plaid shawl for the navy-blue uniform, complete with satin piping, that her daughter (Marita's mother) would don because Marita's grandmother lived her youth before the fifties when public dissemination of information about condoms and diaphragms was legalized and before the sixties when The Pill (momentous enough to warrant capitalization) was invented. Making babies and making money, making life and making a living, it was simply too much of a burden on women in the past, I mused as Marita set off for the ladies' room.

Pleased that I didn't feel in the least bit odd sitting there alone, by myself, I reflected on whether women's political, educational, and material gains abruptly proliferated at the end of the twentieth century because not-just-rich and not-just-famous people no longer had to forfeit lovemaking to attain freedom from maternity, from frequent or often unwanted pregnancies. Still the poorer half of humanity, still woefully unrepresented in political circles, women have nevertheless begun to earn wages nearly equal to those of men. The Pill, birth control, abortion: did these trigger transmutations in sex (the biological manipulation of the body) and in gender (the societal manipulation of the roles of mother, caregiver, nurturer), or was the real basis for change economic, the opening up of virtually all professions to women for the first time in history? In any case, birth control and women's greater employment had driven home the real point behind Wollstonecraft's and Fuller's, Mill's and Schreiner's polemics, their attack on biological determinism, their resistance to the idea that anatomy is destiny, that biology justifies or dictates social norms.

Still, had I detected a note of sadness in Marita's admission that she might not have "any at all"—did she mean children?—or was she simply exhausted by her cobbled-together jobs and the commuting they required? Were there liabilities to the new professionalism if someone as bright as Marita had to forgo or delay the (albeit exhausting) delight of babies? Although more women work outside the home now than ever before and at a greater variety of jobs, what cause for celebration, if they have to accept—either in youth or old age—impossibly arduous, mind-numbing conditions without the benefit of trustworthy, affordable day care? Contemporary women's sacrifices are different from those of their grandmothers and great-grandmothers, but sacrifices they remain, given the sanctity of life (here Max's stash of pocket Bibles popped into my head). Or was Marita not saddened at all, but instead quietly, resolutely relieved at the prospect of getting married and not having to have exhausting (albeit delightful) babies (here Max held out not a Bible but a credit card). Or perhaps she was quietly, resolutely relieved at the prospect of not getting married and of not even having to pretend she wanted to marry or have babies (here Max finally disappeared).

On her return, Marita looked a bit rushed. She had forgotten an appointment to meet Harry on an errand of mercy sponsored by Habitat for Humanity. So, perching a pair of rhinestone-studded sunglasses on the top of her crew cut, she quickly collected her belongings.

"That was a smart point Harry was about to make, don't you think?" I asked, finishing my coffee. "You know, that women no longer need live lives shaped by a sexual division of labor."

"What troubled me was no one processed Nell's objection (she always has something important to add)—that only a very small percentage of women have this sort of freedom, but I wish she had more confidence, spoke up louder."

I needed a minute myself to process what the others hadn't processed and to marvel at Marita's acuity, so I just repeated myself. "I know I shouldn't have been surprised that one of the smartest comments in your class came from a young man, but I was."

In the pause before Marita responded, I would like to believe that I guessed what she was about to say, but then I enjoy thinking well of myself, even—as in this case—when there is absolutely no basis at all for doing so.

"Well, you see," Marita coughed as the reds and the browns of her lovely complexion seemed to rearrange themselves. "Harry is a girl; I mean, Harry was a girl; actually, Harry might be a girl." And then she laughed. "When I first knew Harry," Marita went on to explain, "he, I mean she, was Harriet. Whether or not he'll return to being Harriet, I'm not too clear about."

Was that a sex change or a gender change, I found myself wondering as we parted ways and I walked down a leafy path beyond the Union and my office. Had a surgical procedure occurred or a psychic revolution? Was Harry one of those sickly hermaphroditic "male spirits, confined by mistake in female frames" that Wollstonecraft worried about or a resonantly androgynous incarnation of the "female Newton" (maybe the "male Syren") Fuller forecast? And what did it signify in terms of the intermixing of the sexes in the twenty-first century that a human being could and did vacillate between one sex and the other? No trumpets pealed forth, but truth be told I couldn't for the life of me decide if it mattered one jot that Harry had been a woman, might be so again one day. The fact did nothing whatever to alter his/her identity, her/his perspicacity about "Fantomina," or, for that matter, their dedication to jelly beans. Indeed, Harry had displayed no signs of perturbation at all in the classroom, so why should I worry now that (1) Harriet had been a young woman and (2) that Harry at the moment I met him was a young man?

Striding beyond floating Frisbees and the sleepers, overtaken by joggers and rollerbladers, bicyclists and skateboarders, I determined to think soberly about the perplexities the day had opened up to me, most especially the good old mind/body problem. Should women look to greater forms of liberation by transforming recalcitrant mental attitudes that continue to socialize human beings into one of two types of gender

roles, or should we begin to take seriously those dizzying technologies—of transgenic organisms, hormone therapies, cloning, artificial intelligence—that might obliterate (or revamp)
not only the roles men and women play, not only sexual difference itself, but what it means to be human? Melissa Carmichael would be the friend I would have chosen to thrash out
all these questions—we were engaged in an experiment, team-
teaching that semester; it was she who had been so helpful
when my mother landed in the emergency room—and, though
it is harder to make friends in later life, we were, to my delight,
becoming more than acquaintances or colleagues, for when we
talked, we seemed to vibrate in accord, like stringed instruments. But Melissa and her husband were packing to try out
life on the East Coast, much to my dismay.

Maybe with the help of Marita I could arrange some kind
of conference, a fine way to bring together undergraduates and
graduate students with a few visiting dignitaries who could together profit from the conversations and in the process edu-
cate me and put another entry on Marita's vita. As I passed
by the women's center (named in honor of the intrepid C____
H____) and then through the college gates, I pondered what it
would mean that Mrs. Seton—having flown literally thousands
of travelers around the globe—might now have some money
to leave not only Marita, who wanted to earn a salary (not inherit a legacy), but all of us (whatever that word means); and
what effects that would have on elevators, projectors, and food
courts, but also on the soul (whatever that word means); and
I thought how it is better to move unconstrainedly than to be
penned in or out—better to come and go freely on the campus
of an admittedly dilapidated but relatively cheap school (one

open to Marita and Nimbus, Nell and Harry and, yes, even Arthur) than to be locked in or locked out of the safety and prosperity and privilege accorded only a very few.

Stepping westward to catch a bus (while spotting signs that the redbuds and dogwoods, the pear and apple trees would soon flaunt their resplendent purples, whites, and pinks), I suspected that behind such grandiose speculations lurked more inchoate conjectures: what did the change in Harry's gender? sex? signify about alterations in his sexual desires? Was Harry gay, I wondered, and would that mean he loved the woman he had been or the man she had become? And why was the couple getting into the taxicab at the corner waving at me—the girl (was she a girl?) opening one door, the man (was he a man?) reaching for the other—though I couldn't for the life of me place either one of them? Determined not to be inundated by my own convoluted questionings (or by trepidations that Melissa might not return), as they drove away I hopped off the pavement into the traffic and gestured right back. I was waving, not drowning, I thought, but I was awfully far out.

CHAPTER 2

"THEORY" TROUBLE

_____

It was quite disappointing not to have brought back from the conference some clearer vision of exactly why contemporary thinkers disagree so passionately about gender, sex, and the direction in which feminism ought to be going. For though the months spent with Marita and Nell—inviting speakers, organizing sessions, designing brochures and posters—had raised my expectations, now I felt overwhelmed by an avalanche of opinions from thinkers who disagreed profoundly, many dismissing sex as inconsequential, some deriding gender as insignificant. I wanted the prospect of sawing veal knuckle bones and blanching a calf's foot (neither stocked in my refrigerator) to chase away all thoughts of the presentations, to send me back to a simpler version of the recipe, and the hope that those guests who turned out to be vegetarians would not be offended if—since—there would be glazed carrots and asparagus as well as salads in abundance, to be supplied by generous colleagues amenable to the idea of a potluck. Yet the advocates of gender (alone) and the fewer but fervent advocates of sex (alone) advanced arguments as sticky as the humidity, and the menu hardly seemed suitable, given the season: wouldn't a cold baked salmon—on a bed of parsley, surrounded by lemon slices, sprinkled with capers—look more appetizing, I worried.

A bottle of red wine with a dash of brandy, olive oil, a heavy dose of thyme (more than what was asked for), several bay leaves (though only one was required), three or four mashed garlic cloves, two onions sliced thin: did I have insufficient taste buds, or did the authors of cookbooks pander to pallid palates, I wondered as I vigorously added lots of salt and pepper. Maybe that was my problem, too, during the three days of forums and workshops at the start of the fall term, really two weeks before the beginning of classes and therefore in the blazing heat of the Midwest in August. We had given our speakers (a mix of students, resident faculty, a few visitors—including my dear aunt from Mumbai, Mona Beton) a list of stimulating questions (what a boon for us that Marita extended the invitation at a time Mona was free to relocate her family), but it did not help my wavering powers of concentration that they approached these matters through strangely localized venues, or so it seemed to me. A love poem by Elizabeth Barrett Browning and the history of the Kodak camera, suttee in Indian legal history and transvestism in opera, the disastrous effects of HRT on breast cancer and of slavery on maternity—all fascinating subjects in and of themselves, but nevertheless a curious hodgepodge when considered together.

A very queer composite emerged of what exactly the study of women entails, I sensed as I began to worry about the unsavory presentation of these intriguing topics: why, regardless of the ostensible subject of the speaker, was I being asked to settle on either gender or sex (when they had worked so serviceably together in the past)? That one felt the necessity of choosing had everything to do with the tense atmosphere of people at odds: on one side of the ring, performativity, which had everything to do with playing gender roles for what they were worth; on the other side, those dubbed essentialist, a name they surely would not have picked but that signified their allegiance to the body and its sex. I couldn't make heads or tails of which I would or should choose—indeed, the schism itself felt dated, a reprise from the past—and thus had found myself drifting in a haze of inchoate speculations related less to what was actually being said by the personage behind the podium, more to the timbre of her voice over the drone of the air-conditioning. While others, judging by their ardent note-taking, found enlightenment or, at least, points for debate, I precariously moved along a spider web of speculations only lightly attached to what was going on at the front of the room. Still, I thought, taking leave of the kitchen and making my way to the study, certain phrases and diacritical marks (made by fingers in the air to mimic marks on the page) seemed particularly cloying, for I thought we had moved beyond them.

In the performative camp, those arguing that all aspects of "sex-and-gender" are socially constructed spoke not of selves or individuals, but of "subjects" and "subject positions." Each and every one of these ambiguous "subjects," it seems, was "constituted by discursive practices" or "floating signifiers" that produced (rather than reflected) slippery meanings usually related to French puns (like the jostling of "differ" with "defer" in "*différer*"); or weirdly sinister traps (like "the ruse of regulatory regimes" aiming "to disguise their own genealogies"). Not material conditions but "abysall power/knowledge systems" exercised "panoptic surveillance," apparently making a mockery of people's faith in their ability to understand and shape their own destinies. When other words were put "under erasure" through quotations (like "'woman'"), they somehow seemed inadequate, robbed of reality. If I had never understood structuralism, how could I possibly grasp the utility of post-structuralism, I brooded gloomily as I shuffled through the sheaf of conference presentations (which had been put together in a Xeroxed packet for all the participants).

And it was without a doubt post-structuralism (though it has been vigorously contested by post-post thinkers) that seemed to clog the pages of the gender contingent most alarmingly, at least from my baffled perspective at that moment (and despite my admiration for my aunt; my aunt's esteem for her most formative, formidable friend; and the realization that you may find me as muddled as Marita did then and no doubt still does now). Certainly I comprehended (or thought I comprehended) the politics of critical studies of race or gay culture, but I found myself wondering: what politics could possibly arise from post-structuralism—with its obeisance to all those Frenchmen (like Lacan, Derrida, and Foucault), its arid abstractions (derived from Lacan, Derrida, and Foucault), its smug sense of glamorous sophistication (likewise stemming from Lacan, Derrida, and Foucault, though one by one they were being called away by forces to which or whom they had hardly paid lip service)? How did—did—the sterile intellectual acrobatics of LD&F (like the arcane initials in singles ads) extend the trajectory set by Wollstonecraft, Fuller, and Schreiner, Mill and Taylor, Woolf and Beauvoir—or simply make it look dowdy?

Why were the post-structuralists at the conference suggesting that sex is just as socially constructed as gender, when the sex/gender distinction had managed to derail logic that deems women incapable of standing for the office of president or transforming (confecting was the technical term) the wine to blood, the bread to body within the inner sanctum of churches? Wasn't it exactly the idea that sex rules between the legs, while gender reigns between the ears that enabled Harriet to become Harry so as to bring her primary and secondary sexual characteristics into harmony with his gender identity? Did the name of this "post" movement signal a switch from the creative literature produced by earlier feminist thinkers to dry-as-dust ratiocination (so apt to play one false)? For Wollstonecraft and Beauvoir brought imaginative energies to bear on their speculations; even Fuller considered herself a woman of letters; and Harriet Taylor opted to reside anonymously within Mill's admittedly dull treatises.

But perhaps because these are such difficult questions, ones that might cause me to wander into trackless seas where I would be lost and possibly sunk by huge waves or devoured by sharks, I took a cue from undergraduates who assiduously pursue their research through searches on the Web. At my desk I decided a visit to Amazon.com would provide ballast to offset my vertiginous bewilderment that the relationship between the sexes (or how we approach the problem of the relationship between the sexes) was undergoing a sort of seismic tremor. In pursuit of truth, I wanted to find books that would help me understand how the terms "sex" and "gender" had shifted, and if truth is not to be found on the Internet, where, I asked myself, is truth? Once connected via a password to the modem, I clicked on a bookmark and . . . . . the five dots here are supposed to indicate five separate minutes of stupefaction and wonder.

Have you any notion how many volumes have been written *about men* in the course of the past several years? Have you noticed how many are composed not only by women but also by other men? For centuries, I reasoned as I redirected my search toward books about and by men, women have been the most discussed animal in the universe, but now, it seems, schoolteachers and psychologists, journalists and essayists have provoked a tsunami of serious and prophetic, moral and hortatory words about boys, brothers, husbands, fathers, bachelors, and uncles. Was the influence of Lacan, Derrida, and Foucault at work here, though I had believed their power was diminishing? Hunched before the screen with this query in mind, I had launched my computer search with a poised pencil, but I quickly realized I would need to switch on my printer, which deftly began producing a mass of pages that would fill a folder the size of a rather immodest monograph.

It was vaguely unflattering, I could not help feeling fretfully, to find oneself and one's sex to have been so totally abandoned as an object of attention. To illustrate the troubled mind-set late twentieth-century men brought to a loquacity about masculinity that far exceeded my expectations, I will simply list a few of the works published and sold in the last years of the twentieth century, as they appeared in alphabetical order on the top of my now lowered tray table:

Abused Men (by Philip W. Cook [1997])
Are We Not Men? Masculine Anxiety and the Problem of African-American Identity (by Phillip Brian Harper [1996])

A Circle of Men: The Original Manual for Men's Support
   Groups (by Bill Kauth [1992])
The Decline of Males (by Lionel Tiger [1999])
E-Male: Of Mouse and Men (by Jeff Chacon and Anthony
   Reynoso [1998])
The End of Masculinity: The Confusion of Sexual Genesis and
   Sexual Difference in Modern Society (by John MacInnes
   [1998])
The Fragile Male: The Decline of a Redundant Species (by Ben
   Greenstein [1994])
I Don't Want to Talk about It: Overcoming the Secret Legacy of
   Male Depression (by Terrence Real [1997])
In a Dark Wood: Personal Essays by Men on Middle Age (by
   Steven Harvey [1997])
In a Time of Fallen Heroes: The Re-Creation of Masculinity
   (by R. William Betcher [1999])
Lost Boys: Why Our Sons Turn Violent and How We Can Save
   Them (by James Garbarino [1999])
Male Menopause (by Jed Diamond [1998])
Male on Male Rape: The Hidden Toll of Stigma and Shame
   (by Michael Scarce [1997])
Masculinity: The Hoax Enslaving Men (by Russell S. Dynda
   [1999])
Masculinity in Crisis: Myths, Fantasies and Realities (by
   Roger Horrocks [1994])
My Life as a Male Anorexic (by Michael Krasnow [1996])
Reclaiming Male Sexuality: A Guide to Potency, Vitality and
   Prowess (by George Ryan and Arnold Melman [1997])
Silent Sons: A Book for and about Men (by Robert J. Acker-
   man [1994])
Throwaway Dads: The Myths and Barriers That Keep Men
   from Being the Fathers They Want to Be (by Ross D. Parke
   and Armin A. Brott [1999])

Unheroic Conduct: The Rise of Heterosexuality and the Inven-
tion of the Jewish Man (by Daniel Boyarin [1997])

Violent Land: Single Men and the Social Disorder from the
Frontier to the Inner City (by David T. Courtwright
[1996])

Viropause/Andropause: The Male Menopause Emotional and
Physical Changes Mid-Life Men Experience (by Aubrey M.
Hill [1993])

Walking Wounded: Men's Lives during and since the Vietnam
War (Steve Trimm [1992])

What Men Really Want (by Herb Goldberg [1994])

What Men Want: Mothers, Fathers, and Manhood (by John
Munder Ross [1994])

What Men Want: Three Professional Single Men Reveal What
It Takes to Make a Man Yours (by Gradley Gerstman
[1999])

What Men Want: Why Men Think, Feel and Act the Way They
Do (by H. Norman Wright [1997])

In all the physical and cyberspace bookstores of the world,
the garrulous sex (against common repute) is the male heard
to be talking to himself and, for the most part, about himself, or so I decided when the disengaged modem returned
my wallpaper to the screen, a Cassatt garden scene of women
reading. How odd a flip-flop that Freud's perplexed uncertainty about "what women want" gets repeated so frequently
in the tales Western men tell about themselves. And what exactly had changed that could account for what I feared might
simply reinstate women's historical marginalization? Was the
feminist movement to blame? Did men have to assert their
vulnerability in order to defend themselves against charges
about the misuse of their power in the world? How else to

explain the fragile, menopausal, wounded, anorexic, abused creatures these men felt themselves to be?

But while I pondered these questions I had unconsciously, in my listlessness, been drawing a picture. It was a composite face of French philosophy, though for purposes of simplification I'll call it the figure of Professor de M. engaged in writing his monumental work entitled *The Indeterminacy of "Sexual" Difference.* In my picture he was a man attractive to women, not heavily built, rather pale in complexion, even spectral, but with dark hair just touched by gray, and wearing a beautifully cut black leather jacket, though he looked to be laboring under some anxiety that made him cross out or annotate the words on his paper almost immediately after he wrote them down. As he composed his great tome on the instability of gender hierarchies, the professor looked beleaguered by political institutions and social ideologies that legislate fictive sex roles dangerous to the health and welfare of men as well as women. His work involved "disrupting" or "unraveling," "subverting" or "sabotaging" those "hegemonic dualisms" of "phallologocentrism" that had created an illusion of natural phenomena out of the interplay of "undecidable" signs. Far from being natural, according to Professor de M., "sex" has been constructed "*as if* prediscursive," but needed to be understood as the historical consequence of evolving apparatuses of cultural constructions diffused through schools, prisons, churches, the media, the family, political parties, law courts, and legislation. As for Freud: the unconscious (like everything else) was language; mom was the "not-all"; and dad the *nom du père* or *le non du père*—it was a foreign lexicon to me. Not just "sex" and "mom" and "dad," but "identity" and "women" and "men" should be defined as "regulatory fictions," illusory effects produced by the malignant laws and alluring lores of knowledge and power discourses.

With the body only a symbolic imaginary, the penis only a ghostly phallus, Professor de M. understandably looked a bit nervous, even furtive, though why a person who had received bicoastal institutional positions in the States, a chaired professorship and apartment in Paris, a hefty research account, a bevy of research assistants, and busloads of translators, interpreters, and acolytes should have felt envious or guilty seemed beyond me. Maybe he realized the implications of his own determinism: hadn't he pulled the rug out from under activists? If people cannot speak up but are only spoken through, what political position could possibly be efficacious? This was the problem my friend Melissa called "agency," I recalled, after being startled momentarily by burbling waters through which iridescent fish now swam on my screen saver: "why," she had asked during one of our team-taught classes, "is racial and sexual identity being disparaged at just the moment when African Americans and white women are gaining ground in our struggle for equal rights?" Worse still, Professor de M. appeared to preen himself, seemed to relish his superior insight into the fragility of male privilege, the fictionality of women, as he kept on insisting that "there is no sexual relation" because "woman does not exist" or, curiously enough, because he himself was somehow a woman. And although he kept on assiduously writing, erasing, annotating, and revising his views about the ambiguity and indecipherability of all those categories I was myself trying to understand; although he kept calling for a "playful subversion" of conventional terms, his prose was stymied by hideously abstract postulates going round and around more like agitated gerbils scrambling on an exercise wheel than the phosphorescent flatfish floating through reefs of pink and purple coral on my monitor. So despite my realization that it is indubitably harder to kill a phantom than a reality, I began drawing eyeglasses, a beard, a moustache, and inking every other tooth, until Professor de M. was nothing but a miniaturized version of a desecrated subway poster.

As the motor of a mower started up in a nearby yard, I moved away from the computer, settled into a comfortable chair with a pencil, and ran my eyes up and down the paragraphs of the conference papers, trying to get the hang of what feminists could possibly find useful in Professor de M.'s argument that women are only a figure of speech. Soon it was obvious that something was not quite right. Despite the overhead fan, I warmed with a flush at the influence wielded by one of the most prominent of feminist post-structuralists, my aunt Mona, who argued that sex was not at all natural, but instead only naturalized.

Through a series of eccentric twists and turns in our family's lineage, some time ago Mona had acquired a niece exactly her own age, though we differed in all other respects, for she had an exceptional mental agility I found myself attributing to all Egyptians, not to mention rigorous training that made her almost as much a celebrity in the American academy as Judith Butler, the classmate she had so admired in graduate school and to whose genius she attributed the honing of her own analytic skills; Mona's relocation for a year-long stint at my school would, I hoped, provide me the happy opportunity of renewing our acquaintance. But those who attended the conference because of her advertised name, I fussed as I skimmed the conference essays, are similar to people striking a match that will not light. Why weren't Mary Wollstonecraft's or Olive Schreiner's sentences the right heft or weight for these feminists? Must they all be scrapped, made into orts and fragments, because—yes, there is the idea repeated from Mona's most influential book—because gender, created through reiterated performances, produces only the illusion of a natural sex? While Wollstonecraft and even Schreiner cried out in protest against women's oppression, this obscurity in the conference packet—which so stumped my mind with its prickly references to "the metaphysics of substance" and "the totalizing gestures of feminism" and the "antifoundationalist approach"—might mean Mona's followers were afraid of being called angry or prophetic themselves.

Or perhaps, I added spitefully, mulishly (but with a pang of scruples, for I was very fond of my aunt), they remember that women were thought to be incapable of philosophy and so provide a superfluity of philosophizing. Despite my affection for Mona (and with a spirit troubled by twinges of guilt, or was it resentment?), I fulminated: can I make no sense out of the sentences of post-structuralist feminists because I have been excluded from their audience? Do they write to be taken seriously not by me but by Professor de M., and is this because they are resentful about the insubstantial intellectual fare women have had to ingest in the past; or are my cheeks burning with anger because of a fog of expertise, abstraction, and obscurity meant to make me feel inferior or stupid? Having foresworn the arts of Wollstonecraft and company, Mona Beton and those in her thrall write as men have been taught to write, not as women write, I decided, but just as the red light of rage was flooding the gray cells of reason, the doorbell rang.

At the door stood Nell, juggling a covered dish and laughing at her inability to see through glasses steamed up from the intense humidity.

"What is this?" I asked, peering through the plastic wrap to see the contents of the green ceramic bowl. "I told you *not* to bring anything, there's no need . . ."

"It's not from me," Nell exclaimed, putting the dish down in order to wipe her glasses on the bottom edge of a powder-blue T-shirt imprinted with the tiny letters "girl power" between her breasts. "Mona asked me to bring it for tonight; it's called 'fool.'"

Standing there, the spirit of youth beside the aromatic "fool" in my kitchen, Nell revived thoughts of the dinner to be made, so I asked her to take a seat and give me her reactions to yesterday's sessions, while I sliced the mushrooms and reduced the ripe tomatoes, plucked from the backyard garden, to a bloody pulp.

"Actually, I missed most of it—I was trying to find Chloe; she'd been kind of freaked by this guy, but the two papers I did hear were great," Nell said, sitting down by the table.

"Chloe?" I asked, chopping away at the counter.

"She had finally gotten rid of this creepy guy who had been hassling her."

A jumbled image of a Walkman and fingernails painted in a spectrum of colors hazily arose in my mind as I asked, "Was she the one who walked out early the day I was observing?"

"Could be. She was just auditing," Nell explained, "because she needs all her credits for the pre-med degree. Anyway," she went on, "Chloe, she's my pal, and I hadn't seen her for a few days; though before I started worrying, I did get to Stopes in time to hear an awesome deconstruction of the so-called two sexes."

It was on the tip of my tongue to ask if Chloe was studying AIDS, when intimations of impending and dire circumstances began to alarm me. The Walkman girl obviously wasn't the auditor Marita had missed. Yet just as I began to ask questions about the whereabouts and identity of the "creepy guy," Nell continued.

"I love Anne Fausto-Sterling's idea of adding 'herms' and 'ferms' and 'merms' to the usual suspects. Not just to 'accessorize men and women'"—with these words she raised two fingers of each hand upward toward her ears and bent them twice quickly—"but to deconstruct the binary!"

I then asked Nell whether she had some reservations about all this post-structuralist "deconstruction" of "binaries" (though I noted privately that the propensity to put words into quotation marks was catching). Before she could answer, we were interrupted by a high-pitched refrain of what sounded like "swee too eem oo," and then again "swee too eem oo." She looked startled so I explained about the bird clock on the back porch and pointed her attention to the finches clustered on the feeder just outside the door.

"Look," I said. "The bright yellow fellows are the males and the gray ones the females." I laughed and couldn't help going on. "Now there may be 'herms' and 'ferms' and 'merms' among the finches, too, but they are in short supply."

"You are *so* kidding! Arguing from the birds and the bees never got feminists very far," Nell cautioned, smiling but then becoming more serious. "I get your reservations," she admitted, "but just think how damaging it has been to define humanity in terms of testicles and ovaries . . . or, for that matter, blacks and whites. 'Essentialism'—should be packaged like cigarettes, dangerous to the health of pretty much everyone. Am I black, after all? Is Marita white?"

Even though I was thinking appreciatively of the coppery tones of Marita's skin, of the burnished browns of Nell's, and of how pleased Marita would be at Nell's growing confidence in herself, I protested, wiping the red stain spilling over the cutting board. "But the overwhelming majority of people are born with either male or female genitalia, aren't they, whereas racial categories have no physiological basis at all—why, think of all the people we know who are biracial or mixed."

"Hey, many people wouldn't agree with you there, would see me (more than Marita) as quite apparently, visually different from, for example, you. Besides," she went on, "I have to admit it's not the particular argument that I admire, more like the general skepticism that seems somehow healthy. We *think* we know what the body is, but maybe we just recycle what the culture tells us to believe." She searched for the keys in her purse.

"Thinking about the body as culturally constructed is as difficult as thinking about a kitchen table when you're not there," I grumbled, looking down at my fingers to make sure I hadn't cut myself. But the vegetables were ready so I layered them in the casserole with the whole marinated mass or mess and set it on top of a low flame on the stove.

After Nell cautioned me to refrigerate the "fool" and took her leave, I picked up a plastic timer in the shape of a rooster, twisted its head to the requisite number of minutes, and returned to my study, all too aware of my own few twigs of knowledge: on what intellectual branch could I roost? As I found a copy of one of Mona's publications on my shelves, though, what I was pondering was Nell, so savvy and only a junior. The signal one generation passes to the next must not be cynicism and despair, I felt as I noted that Mona was heaping up too many theorists. She will not be able to do them justice in a book of this size (it was about half the length of *The Second Sex*). However, by some means or other—was it the daunting sophistication of her analyses?—she succeeded in getting me to see some passionate concerns at the heart of her enterprise, as she must have with all those who had thronged to the conference because of her name on our brochure. Wait a minute, I said, leaning back in my chair, I have to consider the whole thing more carefully before I go any further. Had I been merely lazy or conventional in my earlier reaction? Surely it is proper that women should be able to converse with Professor de M. in and on his terms, for there is no man's sentence unsuited for a woman's use, and Mona must be commended, not criticized, for refusing to be kept off the philosophic turf, or so I determined as the drone of the mower ceased (the ensuing silence seeming to usher in the mingled fragrance of newly cut grass and honeysuckle, along with the peaceful sound of the still burbling tank on the screen).

In the midst of these reflections, while I determined to do my duty by the post-structuralists as a reader if they would do their duty by me as feminist thinkers, I turned the pages and read— I am sorry to break off abruptly here, but you who are holding me in your hands: you wouldn't consider yourself

a neo-con, a right-winger, and you didn't support the framing of the "don't ask, don't tell" policy, or seek to outlaw the
teaching of Charles Darwin, did you? You never contributed a
penny to the campaigns of Phyllis Schlafly, Jerry Falwell, Jesse
Helms, Newt Gingrich, Pat Robertson, or Tom DeLay? We are
all feminists, you assure me?

Then I may inform you that certain words seemed to lend
Mona's abstractions a driving propulsion: she wanted to demonstrate how "women"—more than most "subjects"—have
been "subjected" to debilitating cultural definitions that programmed them to fatten or starve themselves, to renounce
their desire for professional ambition as crazy or sick but
embrace their desire for men or children or God as sane or
healthy. If the quotation marks around "women" would allow
them to adopt a range of positions, not all of them coherent or
consistent; if "women" were not simply the devalued opposite
of "men," this did not mean that Mona doubted their existence;
but she did cast doubt on any claims one might make about who
they are or must be, and what they might become. Aren't there,
she seemed to ask, as many differences among women as there
are differences within a single, particular woman?—a question
I had to answer in the affirmative, for I knew how many various people had lodgment at one time or another within me so
that, when sick to death of one particular self, I often felt the
need to call upon another, but sometimes, less in command
of myself, I simply encountered a new embryo self at the next
corner, waiting near an adjacent landing. And if these presences of which each "woman" or "man" are built up, one on
top of another like plates piled on a waitress's hand, have complicated and diverse needs and wishes, then of course we re-

ally must move beyond those neat compartments we put men and women into, thereby leaving the physically fixed body and possibly heterosexuality, too, in a storm cloud of dust.

Mona was getting at the preeminence of the culturally constructed psyche over a decidedly malleable body—yes, it explained something about Fantomina, whose masquerades illustrate how we all impersonate the multiple roles we play; and about Harry, whose mental conception of himself took precedence over a process that proved how his body could be reconfigured. I must give Mona her due since weren't some proportion of infants born with ambiguous genitalia and didn't a significant percentage of people display chromosomal variations that ought not be stuffed into the XX-female and XY-male boxes? For the majority of middle-class Americans, as well, bodybuilding, no less than tanning devices; contact lenses, no less than prosthetic limbs, liposuction, nose jobs, breast augmentation, buttocks implants, tummy tucks, collagen injections, organ transplants, Prozac and Zoloft, pacemakers, hair-generating potions, "double-eyelid" surgery, Botox, joint replacements, steroids, fertility procedures, phalloplasty and penile augmentation (John Bobbitt's boons)—all attest to the plasticity (Mona would say the "discursive performativity") of the material body shaped by minds very much conditioned by historically evolving cultures. How we define, diagnose, and treat illness, whose bodies we view as models of health or beauty—these surely are products of judgments saturated by TV, Hollywood films, diet fads, gym and food and drug industries, fashion magazines, video games, and, of course, Barbie dolls.

And wasn't it the mind, after all, which tyrannical governments and bigoted despots sought (often successfully) to control (I thought of brain-washing, *The Manchurian Candidate*, Salem witch trials), turning human beings into mere automatons? For this reason, I speculated as I enlisted as a sort of accomplice in Mona's mission, hadn't some of the greatest women artists before post-structuralism tried to describe the world seen without a self? What sin in history hadn't the sovereign self been found guilty of committing, I conceded. By questioning the autonomy of the individual, the coherence and independence of the ego, didn't the post-structuralists dismantle the pride, the possessiveness, the arrogance so many earlier feminists had seen in the patriarchal "I"? Like a straight iron bar, hadn't men's needs and desires been used to justify their domination of other men with slightly different complexions or gods, of women, and of the natural world (of birds, beasts, and flowers)? One begins to be tired of "I," Mona seemed to be saying. Not but that this "I" was a most respectable "I"; honest and logical; as hard as a walnut, if not always polished by good breeding. But, Mona warned, nothing will grow in the aridity cast by its shadow, for it had produced war after war in the name of its magisterial supremacy, disaster after disaster under the banner of its assertive virility. (Here frightful images of shivering skeletons in striped uniforms, of a mushroom-shaped cloud arose in my mind's eye.)

The rampant individualism of that "I," Mona cautioned, demanded grist for its mill of making an elite cadre of men feel superior, and what were the ideas of "sexed" or "raced" bodies or "gendered species" except such narcotic, addictive, hallucinogenic grist? For the "I" insisted on a "you" that penned in people categorized as "Jews" or "blacks" or "women" and thus forced to respond by either disclaiming or claiming, resisting or espousing a "Jewishness" or "blackness" or "femininity" that thereby kept them captive. To do away with identity categories would mean cutting those phantasmagoric but not therefore less powerfully wired cords and fences. Don't we have more than enough ghettos as is? Besides, if an explorer should bring word of other sexes or species looking through the branches of other trees, could anything possibly be a greater service to the human race? In any case, I thought, couldn't humanity be defined by less-sickening words?

Not just sex and identity, also sexuality; that is, the barriers between "homosexuals" and "heterosexuals." For Mona, I realized, cantering beyond sex means escaping the terrain Adrienne Rich called "compulsory heterosexuality," galloping into a realm where straight people cannot relegate gay people to an imitation of or deviation from the norm, where the very terms "gay" and "straight" cease to contain or constrain people whose behaviors and feelings cannot be so easily categorized. With sexuality no longer immutable or stable, gender was made into a verb by the post-structuralists, an active word "re-signifying" what one may do, instead of a static noun fixing who one needs to be. Some idea of a new form of humanity surely inspired the post-structuralist effort to imagine what had never been experienced, a genderless or multiply gendered society. Not even a feminist theorist schooled by Professor de M. can say for certain what the words "emancipation" or "liberation" amount to, but energy has been freed by this attempt to break the usual sequences of our thinking and, I wondered, into what forms would it, should it flow? My aunt wrote as a woman who has determined to forget that she is a woman, I realized, and therefore her pages are full of that

curiously convoluted trait that comes when sex strives to be
unconscious of itself. Nor was she alone in this endeavor. As
different as Julia Kristeva and Hélène Cixous are from Judith
Butler; as different as Gayatri Spivak is from Donna Haraway
or, for that matter, from Martha Nussbaum, Alison Jaggar,
Rosi Braidotti, Genevieve Lloyd, and Seyla Benhabib: together they have transformed what one might have taken to be the
fixed trajectory of philosophizing. Thus, toward the end of the
twentieth century, a change came about which, if I were writing
intellectual history, I should think of greater importance than
the Vietnam, Falkland Islands, and Gulf Wars. Middle-class
women began to exert a significant impact on the writing and
teaching of philosophy.

The insistent buzz of the rooster informed me it was time
to move the pot from the top of the stove to the oven, so I put
Mona's book back on the shelf, switched off the fish tank, gath-
ered my packet of papers, and returned to the kitchen. It was
pointless to tell myself not to worry about the house burning
down in my absence, I knew as I checked to be sure the oven
temperature was low, locked the back door, and glanced at the
flower bed beneath a shady beech tree. "That is not whole,"
I said to myself about the nibbled edges of the hosta's bitten
leaves, while I made my way quickly down the tree-lined street.
A few other pedestrians daring the glare and heat of the midday
sun seemed bound on private affairs that would quickly usher
them back into the cooler indoors, but I was so sunk in thought
that I barely noticed them. Who we are and how we know ourselves to be who we are cannot easily be disentangled, I agreed
with Mona. Was I laboring under the illusion of being an actual, real woman, I wondered, though I knew illusions to be

the most valuable and necessary of all things? Regardless—"ir-regardless," my students sometimes said—of Mona's explicit wish to eroticize all sorts of liaisons (and perhaps because I finally felt at peace after the painful breakup of a long-term relationship), it was exhilarating for me to believe that there is no single characteristic common to all women, that libera-tion from the category of sex might mean emancipation from sexuality; to deem heterosexuality just as outré as homosexual-ity is quite refreshing, I determined, watching a dignified but extremely frail old lady pausing at the corner to avoid collision with a helmeted biker who brandished in one upraised hand a bouquet of lilies. For, at this time in my life, the conflagration of desire (of any sort) appalled me. All those fires flaring and flaming between two people scorched in the heat of love, the crackle of its cruelty, simply the stupidest, the most barbaric of human passions and so nice to be exempted, not to have to undergo that particular degradation. (Here I glanced down at my ringless fingers.)

But why does Mona (I was still brooding on post-struc-turalism) endorse the idea of modeling my feminine perfor-mance on the drag queen? (Here the elderly woman—absorbed in her business of placing her feet so as to avoid stray cracks in the pavement—proceeded to cross the street alongside me.) She (my aunt, not the intrepid marcher) wants to say that sex (like gender) is a routine, but I vaguely recalled that the one drag show I had personally witnessed (in San Francisco) ended with the female impersonator displaying his genitals, a finale meant to emphasize the fictitiousness of femininity when acted by a person with the turkey neck and gizzards Sylvia Plath had dared to laugh at in *The Bell Jar*. Yes, femininity had become a performance, but the penis-on-display then took on the resonance of the real. As the tenacious lady abruptly parted ways by turning toward the shops in town, I severely scolded myself (she could not possibly have seen the staged scene I was visualizing). Yet I felt myself nevertheless falling from the rarefied world of reflection into the mundane consideration of locating the auditorium in the biology building where conference participants were assembling before the last sessions of the day.

Delightfully cool and dimly lit, the corridor I entered was one of my favorite places on campus, lined, on the right side, with glass cabinets containing the stuffed or varnished remains of sinuous snakes, intricate mollusks, striated starfish, and mosaic-backed turtles (some within fluid-filled jars) and, on the left side, with sketches done in colored pencils of brown, gray, yellow, and red birds perched on the branches of trees or nesting on eggs in bushes. "You can make white-tufted sparrows learn other birds' songs," I recalled one earnest colleague explaining about singing, which is mostly restricted to or superior in males, "but they will not produce them as well as their own calls or the songs' original singers." "How can you *make* them?"—I had objected not so much on the basis of my usual loathing of the forcing, the bullying I always fear and dread, but really as a practical question; "simply by confining them to the company of birds of another family," the ornithologist had explained at a president's tea (where Melissa and I had described our scheme for team-teaching to other faculty interested in such a venture).

Just the other day, another colleague had begun a presentation with the point that the scientists working on the human genome project have established that we share 98 percent of our chromosomes with the chimpanzees. "We are awash with hormones, neurotransmitters, cortisols, and mitochondrial predispositions," she had declared. Does what she called the "leftover 2 percent" also obey physiological axioms? What would the post-structuralists make of the fact that some of the scientists not experimenting with flies, rats, ducks, and rhesus monkeys in this very building study the effects of the bulging bridge tissue connecting the two brain hemispheres in women (the corpus callosum) as well as their higher levels of estrogen and oxytocin, all of which (they believe) lend women verbal facility (girls speak earlier, use more complex constructions, stutter less frequently) and facilitate greater emotional responsiveness in later life (blessing some with greater empathy, cursing others with more depression)? Did brain chemistry account for the fact that 80 percent of autistic people are male? Because men have some seven-to-ten times more testosterone than women, do they exhibit far greater degrees of competitiveness and aggression?

Though even the faintest allusion to hunters and gatherers makes me queasy, statistically speaking (I had to admit) hyperactive kids tend to be male, as do the fastest sprinters, the strongest weight-lifters, the most powerful ball-throwers, the fiercest soldiers, the more promiscuous partners, the vast preponderance of terrorists and of inmates waiting for a reprieve on death row. Whether or not evolution was to blame—why assume all sperm-producing hunters were polygamous? all ego-protective gatherers monogamous females?—morphology (the nerves that feed the brain may differ in men and women) plays a part in our constitutions, I conceded, thinking about all the ills flesh is heir to (Down syndrome, sickle-cell anemia, Tay-

Sachs or Gaucher disease). For (I argued with Mona) Harry's discomfort at the mismatch between his body and his sense of self—his no doubt painful hormone therapy, surgical removal of organs, and grafting of new parts—proved his investment in his own fleshly corporeality. And just as he could not engender offspring who would inherit his genetic code, it was pregnancy that put a stop to Fantomina's female impersonations. Even if select women decide to anoint themselves daily with AndroGel, even if certain men nightly imbibe doses of Estra-Pro, most people are driven by female and male hormones that explain why separate but equal sporting events continue to be funded by well-intentioned members of the university athletic committee who understand that all but a few (highly unusual) women cannot possibly compete with men in integrated tennis matches, soccer leagues, and hockey tournaments.

Under some circumstances (here I addressed my aunt Mona rather severely), it would be sexist to ignore biological differences between men and women. In the "olden days" (as my students put it) but also intermittently now, indeed right here at the conference, this was what was called "difference feminism": not equality for women, but a recognition, celebration, and guarding of their particular strengths and needs. Ought not education fortify the divergences rather than the similarities between the sexes? In direct opposition to the post-structuralists, these feminists emphasized how all aspects of "sex-and-gender" are biologically inflected by natural differences. As I turned a corner in the cavernous building, here lined with cases containing skeletons of small mammals, I considered the arguments of feminist ethicists (like Carol Gilligan and Sara Ruddick) that women—by virtue of physiological

functions or an upbringing related to their daughterly or maternal capacities—were more nurturing and cooperative, more
intimately connected to the natural world and to each other,
more fluid and accepting of ambiguity, less judgmental or universalizing in their conceptualizing of social interaction.

And it was true, I granted, that the pairs of friends—did
men have comparable friendships?—I invariably encountered when buying tomato plants and potted herbs at the difficult to find but wonderfully named Burnham Woods Nursery
were disproportionately female, though I had seen more men
when (on my last trek out there) I needed to purchase deer re-
pellent, the also wonderfully named Not Tonight Deer. Buck
and doe: didn't the average human female weigh ten pounds
less than the average male, who exhibits less body fat, more
muscle, a greater amount of hair on his body, superior height
(and less willingness to ask directions)? Weren't there always
longer lines at the women's bathrooms during intermission
(they didn't call it that) at popular sporting events? To the
post-structuralists' charge of essentialism, such difference
feminists would retort, "There can be a great deal of diversity
among objects of the same class, be they deer or women, and
yet men will be men, women, women (deer, deer), variations
in kind notwithstanding." But separate rarely did mean equal,
I sighed as I swung open the door at the end of the hall, thinking of the poor turnout at the women's basketball games, despite a series of protests that had managed to persuade the administration to keep concession stands open during the girls'
tournaments.

At the front of the darkened amphitheater crowded with
all sorts of participants wearing name badges, Mona Beton

stood before a screen with two projected slide diagrams, but had I missed the presentation itself (I worried)? No, dressed in a diaphanous pink, red, and gold sari, she was ignoring a cell phone going off at the rear of the room (somewhere in my vicinity), using a state-of-the-art laser pointer to gesture toward the first equation, which looked like a circuit with arrows linking the three aspects of what she proceeded to call an outmoded model of cognition: an arrow from the word WORLD led to the word BRAIN, which in turn had an arrow pointing to the word BODY, which had an arrow circling back to the word WORLD. Yet just as I was about to settle down to listen, Harry rushed over and whispered in my ear that I should follow him. Despite my protestations, he urged me to hurry out of the auditorium and then directly across the hall into an adjacent cluttered room, the now largely vacated book exhibit, and since he looked distraught, I quickly complied. Stacks of all sorts of volumes, some by conference participants and some not, were being sold, along with T-shirts, silver pendants, and posters; yet because Mona was famous (not for her early work on equestrian kinesiology, but for her subsequent research on epistemology—though why one had led to the other remains a bit of a mystery), most people had gone to the auditorium to hear her lecture.

"Don't be upset," Harry was murmuring, as he managed to find two chairs free of books and move them to the far corner of the huge room under a capacious stained-glass window. The words sent a chill through me, though maybe that was just the effect of his evident distress and the strenuous air-conditioning.

"What? Why?" I felt flustered, sitting down beside him.

"Don't be upset, but something is wrong," Harry began, as one of his legs (as if on its own accord) started to jitter up and down. He wore a badge that identified him as a Conference Facilitator. "Chloe is missing. Her hat was found on Harley Lane, you know, that trail by the lake. The police are investigating."

"Oh, my God," I exclaimed. "Hadn't someone been bothering her? What could have happened?" My throat constricted, recalling Nell's and then Marita's earlier concerns.

"She was supposed to be helping with registration yesterday, but she never showed up," Harry said, looking anxious, his leg going faster. "That's when Nell started to try to track her down, even asked at the shelter because she'd been getting these horrible phone threats. When she didn't turn up again this morning, I called around . . . no results, which wasn't like her—she knew I was depending on her. So I biked to her place at noon, but she wasn't there." He slumped over and pushed his hands against the top of his head, as both legs now pumped.

"I hadn't realized they were actual threats. So we don't know exactly how long she's been missing? How do you know about the hat?" I started to feel a kind of trembling not exactly inside but all over and around me.

"I finally broke down and contacted the police," Harry said, lifting his head up with difficulty. "They had just found it . . . couldn't have been more than two or three hours ago; the story will appear in tomorrow's paper. But I got the feeling they weren't telling me all that they found, you know, at the scene . . . they clearly had begun some sort of investigation."

Horrible headlines from the newspaper ran through my head, a sinister band of very large capitals across the front page—WIFE MURDERED, HUSBAND KILLS SELF—followed by dreadful accounts: a machete with human blood on it had been found in a cellar. But I forced myself to say, "Phone them again, Harry. There are plenty of people here who knew—I mean, must *know*—Chloe. Go see if they can send someone over. Go now; I'll wait here."

As Harry rushed off, relieved to be given something to do, I realized I could have made the call myself, but felt the need for some time apart, alone and quiet. Cold and yet clammy, I put on the linen jacket draped over my arm as I glanced around at the stacks of biographies of Marie de France, Lou Andreas Salomé, and Catharine Beecher; recovered diaries and journals of medieval saints and Irish revolutionaries; histories of wealthy women in Classical Rome, Renaissance England, and eighteenth-century China; of Victorian and contemporary women in politics, science, and the law; a mass of information from parish registers and settlement houses about working-class marriages and domestic employment and childbearing and child-rearing practices; the collected music of Clara Schumann and paintings of Artemisia Gentileschi; the poems of Sappho and Juana Inez de la Cruz; the prose of Murasaki Shikibu and accounts of the establishment of Native American schools for girls: what did it all amount to?

We had rewritten history, found and recorded the lives of the obscure as well as the eminent, filled the empty shelves with tomes of rare worth so as to make our knowledge of the past less lopsided. And exactly what had we effected with our thousands of pens embarked upon this laborious and highly productive campaign? We had published all sorts of books, hesitating at no subject, however trivial or however vast. Nor were our efforts limited to the academic sphere. We had sponsored legis-

lation making it possible for nannies to build bridges, sales-
girls to drive buses, seamstresses to fight fires or mine coal; we
had elected judges enforcing that legislation, enabling mothers to become soldiers or attorneys or dock laborers: the Equal
Pay Act, Title IX, the Family and Medical Leave Act.

But had our research and activism resulted in our own good
or the good of the world at large? The television newscasters
declare that the vast proportion of Americans living below the
poverty line are older women and young mothers with dependent children; no culprit has been found for the slaying of the
five-year-old beauty pageant princess in Colorado; the sena-
tor cannot get legislation for welfare recipients passed; a doctor and administrator at Planned Parenthood have been shot;
a pair of boys bomb their own high school; a serial killer goes
on a spree in the Southwest; another military wife is dragged
up to a barrack room at Fort Bragg and thrown upon a bed;
pimps prostitute twelve-year-old girls at the Mall of America.
And the newspaper banners announce Islamic women in Bos-
nia were systematically raped by Serbian soldiers; the body of
the founder of the Revolutionary Association of the Women of
Afghanistan was never recovered. The most transient visitor
to the globe, who picks up or turns on the news, could not fail
to be aware, even from this scattered testimony, that civiliza-
tion remains under a rule hostile to the health and welfare of
humanity.

Nobody in their senses could fail to detect the dominance
of man. He owned the paper as well as the network and dot-
com, with the political influence they confer. He refused to
fund child-care centers and public education in the inner cit-
ies; stockpiled "defensive" arsenals of nuclear warheads; cov-

ered up toxic waste in the property and produce he advertised;
manufactured cigarettes at great profit and marketed them
throughout the third world; and "managed" health care, lying
about medical malpractice. The homeless sit at the corner of
the same city block where he—a devotee of the stock exchange,
the bond market, the Nasdaq, the Standard and Poor's index—
obeys the commands of the vulture in his breast, which incites
him to make more money and then again more money until his
annual income sounds like a long distance phone number. (It
was he who would determine whose blood was on the machete.)
Bowed down in trepidation, I muttered, teach your daughters a
lament and their neighbors a dirge, for death has come up into
our window. Instantly annoyed, I felt as if I had been trapped
into saying something I did not believe and so gave myself a
little shake as Harry returned, nodding assurances, presumably that the police would soon appear.

"They'd like us to gather together everyone who has been
with her in the past few weeks or months," Harry reported.
"Want to find out any background information that might be
useful."

"Did Chloe often go running by herself?" I asked, not
wanting to sound censorious.

"She loved the path by the lake. Sometimes Nell would go
with her, but she liked going alone, too." Harry explained that
the coach of the running team had given solitary joggers all
sorts of tips on how to handle menacing dogs, or hostile strang-
ers on foot or wheels, that Chloe was exceptionally fit and knew
how to take care of herself. "She did everything right," he assured me over and over again, as if to convince himself that all
would be well.

After a brief discussion, we determined to make an announcement at the end of Mona's question-answer period, telling people who knew Chloe or wanted to help the police to reassemble at the front of the room and encouraging the rest to go to the smaller sessions that were supposed to follow. We hadn't expected most of the audience to stay, but they did, as if stunned by the dreadful announcement: campus officers introduced detectives who had conducted forensic work on evidence they could not divulge, but it had given them cause to believe Chloe endangered. Because I was up on the stage myself with a policeman, Harry, and Marita, all the lights and hubbub and talk made it hard for me then to take it in, hard for me now to reconstruct events as they must really have occurred. What I recall remains painfully partial, exasperatingly subjective, but we must make do with what we have, I suppose, so imagine the overhead lights brightened, the banked tiers of upholstered seats filled in a lecture hall that grew increasingly crowded and noisy, a microphone toward the back in a central aisle and another on the stage, the chagrin growing as if fanned by certain synthetic drafts wafted about by the air conditioning, fumbling gusts brushing the walls, nibbling at the corners, suffocating the seated as well as the standing, breeding consternation, hollowing out optimism and faith until it seemed the entire auditorium was rocked in brute confusion and tumultuous rage.

Amid the lapping and licking of these agitating currents, only a few moments—sometimes only a phrase or two—stand out as if contoured by the breathlessness they induced, for I was struggling for a ghastly sort of anesthetization by trying to make some sense of the skein of what had turned out to be a sordid, miserable day. Retrospectively, it might seem heart-less—of course feminist debates had nothing to do with Chloe's calamitous fate—but that was just the point: it was a way of feel-ing heartless, of feeling nothing whatsoever. Not feeling was preferable to those unreal emotions predictably enacted when one is being observed. If Melissa were present, the comfort of confiding my fears might have helped me better cope, but alone I tried to numb myself; what the policeman said—"last seen at," "incriminating evidence," "family informed"—was blown about by the remorseless waves of air beating about the room, defying questions and explanations, procedures and plans. While he filled in background information to account for Chloe's disappearance—"a counselor at the shelter last month"—I tried to keep myself from visibly gasping by un-tangling "testosterone" from "discursive performativity," so-called "essentialism" from "social constructionism." He was bombarded with questions—"a reward for information"—but the twitching and tossing that threatened to empty words of their meaning seemed to intimate that men had always, would always harm women. Engines of a violence that had stained history for centuries, they deserved to land on death row.

After the police left the stage, a woman standing in the aisle made an impassioned speech, citing Catharine MacKin-non and Andrea Dworkin, targeting male dominance, female submission in incest, sexual harassment, rape, prostitution, pornography, spousal abuse, and pederasty. Snatches of her words—"*Silence of the Lambs,*" "'wildings' in Central Park," "'honor' murders"—accompanied my fearful dread that per-haps this was what physiological differences between the sexes amounted to, for women have rarely done unto others what has for so very long been done to them. Some people in the audience clearly resented the translation of Chloe into a case history (not to mention the didactic, the loudspeaker tone), but my attention was taken up by the effort to brace myself against the buffeting gusts. Considering the shocking statistics with which another speaker concluded—"a rape occurs every six minutes in the United States; 44 percent of rape survivors are under the age of eighteen"—I fretted: what possible difference would it make to determine why Chloe was gone since I believed she was irretrievably lost to her friends, her family, and to what fearsome state I could not let my mind consider. Women, no longer the protected sex, only die off so much younger in these seemingly progressive times, I brooded.

The person who rescued me from the impending turbulence, steadied my breathing, made an impression not simply because she was a particular friend of mine. An activist responsible for running the women's studies program on campus, Evelyn Hamilton was a portly woman, as comfortable as the soft cardigan she wore over a flowing sundress, glowing with flesh-and-blood earthiness, self-assured, and bent on doing something, anything. Warmth somehow permeated her being, cushioned the cold contact of man and woman, or of women together. If anyone could quiet the tumbling and tossing, it was Evie—so plainspoken and downright, though a full decade younger than I—or so I briefly intuited as my whole being (all of a sudden, as if inspired by the sight of her) rose up against all explanations of Chloe's fate that would in any way carve it in perpetuity or exonerate the evil that had produced it, as sociobiologists did. Since I concurred with what I had once read, that the seed of a theory consists of the desire to prove what the theorist wishes to believe, Nell's hunch in the kitchen, I felt now, provided a spool on which to wind the tangled yarn of my day.

Impossible, it seemed to me, to accept the idea that men will always kill women, though it may have happened yesterday or today here in my own small place on the planet. Finches notwithstanding, at the very least Mona would not doom us (and by "us" I meant men as well as women) to accept such a dreadful sentence. For even if the body is not entirely or merely a discursive construct, my aunt was indubitably right—how we understand it is infiltrated by the cultural, the "conditioned" air we inexorably breathe. And how it is apprehended and treated has been grotesquely shaped by societies forgetful that men and women have more in common with each other than with birds, beasts, and flowers. Don't we all start out as identical zygotes for the first six weeks of development, I lectured myself, and don't we share the same external genitalia for the first eight weeks of fetal life as well as the same hormones thereafter, though in different quantities? Hadn't I read somewhere that women with AIS (androgen insensitivity syndrome) have a Y chromosome as well as temperaments that disprove the idea that testosterone is the "hormone of aggression"? The physiological facts of genetics may inflect intelligence, personality, disability, sexual orientation, but insisting on their primacy or priority will only harm those committed to promoting social justice. If I had to choose between gender and sex, I decided then and still believe now, better to embrace a theory consisting of the desire to prove what feminists have always wished to believe, that fear and bitterness can modify themselves into pity and toleration; and then again, pity and toleration might go, ushering in the greatest release, into the freedom to think and live without fear or pity.

What had been done to Chloe, after all, has absolutely no analogue among finches or, for that matter, flies, rats, or monkeys, no matter what scientists claimed, and hadn't they argued for centuries that the vagina was just an internalized penis and later that cranial measurements proved the stupidity of women? My soul rebelled against any recourse to biology that would be used to suggest that women were somehow physiologically programmed for receiving, men for inflicting pain. The women I knew did not view heterosexuality as an oppressive institution requiring female erotic submission. Nor, I thought—considering Harry as well as the two men I most trusted on the faculty—would it be reasonable to equate all forms of male sexuality with a pernicious drive for supremacy. To still the cacophony in my head, I made a concerted effort to hold the air in my lungs while reminding myself that such ideas hurt people so very fragile in our common vulnerabilities to each other, since weren't many of the inmates on death row African American, not because of higher levels of testosterone, but because of a vicious social order that either judged them guilty until proven innocent or brutalized them?

It was reassuring to turn my attention to the strength that seemed to flow from Evie. The vigor of her attitude roused me, made me want to remember that (somehow maternal, though she had no children) she called herself a "justice-seeker," for she had suffered as a child—could recite exactly what measly portions of frozen vegetables, tinned meats were offered the six kids in her family every night of the week, while her parents ate abundant, choicer foods at a separate table—and therefore against all odds Evie ended up wanting to give as much as or maybe more than she received. Her legacy was enormous, making the academy much more hospitable to women, whether or not they were feminists, and to a host of students: Marita had informed me that it was Evie who had helped Harry make peace with his parents. To me, personally, Evie seemed to be saying that ultimately the theoretical arguments will and should run their course; but in the short term, we must save this particular girl from further suffering.

"The making of a martyrdom is the last thing Chloe would want," she exclaimed, magnificent in her unselfconsciousness. Not pausing for assent, though she was clearly getting it, Evie began to outline steps groups of concerned people could take: getting photos of Chloe; putting them on a poster with descriptions of her height, weight, complexion, eye color, age; plastering it on the churches, storefronts, and banks in town; setting up a hotline with the police; tying yellow ribbons around flagpoles and trees on local country roads; obtaining radio and TV spots. As the audience began working out with her the details of various activities, Evie—drawn up to her full height—somewhat stilled the rollicking currents, or was that effect simply produced by the slow disbanding of conference participants to their appointed tasks?

Why did so many around me seem discernibly heartened by her words and the jobs set before them, I wondered, whereas (despite my concerted efforts and the tonic of Evie's courage and candor) I still gasped for breath, picturing Chloe wedged like a log in the muck at the bottom of the lake, thrown like garbage into a ragged ditch by the side of the road, or beaten and flung about a room, penned up and tormented in some way that made my mind go blank? Dispersed are we, I repeated as I tried to banish the images, to surface from the brutal dousing that had aimlessly coursed over me during that afternoon and so reasoned: such agonies of different sorts have to be faced periodically, for they, too, pertain to the situation of women at the present time, though one wants not to face them but to reject, resist, destroy them and thus find acceptance on new terms, with rapture. Yet even such a decidedly healthy effort as that denoted by reaching for the word "rapture" thudded in my ears, now plugged by the drench and drone of "shelters" and "rewards." What had gone wrong with men that they could do such things, I wondered, longing for an antidote to my anguished state. And though such a question could not but be contaminated by precisely the echoes of female victimization I had set my life's work against, it would not go away, as I realized it might be some time before I could return home, where no dinner party would transpire, no toasts, no guests, no conviviality, no "fool," only a pot that would have to be taken from the oven, cooled on the counter, and (if not ruined) then stored away in the freezer for better days.

CHAPTER 3

WHITE LIKE ME

THE SCENE, if I may ask you to follow me, was now not only changed but changing before my eyes, as I brooded over what might have been a wild goose chase. While I looked down through the oval plastic portal at the uproar of the city—the bustle of the crowded streets dwarfed by towering skyscrapers, the roar of jackhammers punctuated by horns blaring from yellow cabs first gridlocked, then hurtling between potholes and parked trucks and streaking silver scooters—the vast, noisy workshop that had been New York was simply a mute island growing smaller. Attached by the filaments of numerous bridges to other floating land masses, it shrank silently in the vast expanse of the gray Atlantic's waves as it dropped away. When I shifted my gaze, the parks and shops that attract as well as the garbage and grime that repulse, the museums and restaurants that delight as well as block after block of horrifying slums disappeared in the downfall of the sky, the billowing clouds and haze now making even the wing tip itself evaporate, dissolve into nothing but a flashing light.

The inevitable sequel to the weeks, then months that brought no knowledge of Chloe's fate was only a memorial service, and then a fund-raising drive jointly organized with the hospital (because she had been a dedicated and prized volunteer there). Day after day we had wanted to believe that some explanation would arrive in the mail, that she was safe and sound. Chloe, we urgently needed to convince ourselves, couldn't have been snatched from us, from a protective campus environment, and without our knowing where, how, by whom, or exactly when. Yet this dreadful thing had happened—the blow of a treachery, a betrayal; it struck on her friends, each hopelessly passive under the sledgehammer of grief, exposed and unprotected, with nothing to ward it off. Strained of whatever was personal or accidental in it (much of which remained shrouded in mystery because the abusive stalker had vanished), Chloe's disappearance had spawned a swarm of questions, even for those (like me) who had not known her and who now feared they would never get to know her.

Although American and European women have voted for more than eighty years; although we have entered most of the professions over the course of the past half century; although we have gained some reproductive rights and served in the army, navy, and air force for several decades; although a few exceptional women have attained leadership roles in a minuscule number of governments, religions, and industries in the last couple of years—why was one sex still so much more powerful than the other, and why was this more prosperous sex more vindictive than and toward the other? Could it be that the tenacity of men's opposition to women's emancipation will trip every step forward into a staggering fall backward? Caught within the rhythms of backlash, are men destined to fear that our gains are their losses? Or is it wrong, I could not help but interrupt myself, to generalize about an injury that might just be attributable to the inexplicable perversity of one very twisted person's grotesque obsession with a girl whose loss would so grieve her parents, teachers, and friends? You can see that, despite the buffeting, I was trying to keep steady in my mind the concerns with which I began: what sorts of advances have been made by the multiplied feminisms that morphed through our recent lives and times, and for—as well as by—which women?

Amid the untimed maneuvers of impermanent clouds, I mulled over these perennial puzzles, as Emma Lazarus's colossal lady faded from view, along with the dispiriting gap where the twin Trade Center towers had been when the unthinkable occurred and loaded passenger planes had been turned into incendiary instruments of destruction, inflicting a wound without precedent on the majesty of New York's skyline and also on the national psyche. Here, but on an unimaginable, inconceivable scale, the impossible had happened—the blows of treachery, betrayals of gigantic proportions, a succession of explosions struck people horrified, solemn, and unreal under a haze of baffled emotions. First the bellowing eruptions against a picture-perfect blue sky, the debris and ashes, people leaping out of windows, their rescuers trapped; then the shimmering skeleton of the second tower as it collapsed over again and again on televised replays: on or about September 11, many commentators immediately noted, a catastrophic shock shifted human relations—those between human beings on this side of the globe and human beings on the other side of the globe. And when human relations change there is at the same time a shift in politics and religion, public commerce and private conduct, education, and, of course, feminism as well.

With the Hudson and East Rivers replaced by a foggy sky obscuring mountain ranges the first inhabitants of the continent must have scouted, I pondered the connection between the virulent misogyny of the terrorists (whose fundamentalism—should it take hold—would virtually enslave the women of their native lands) and their acts of violence against civilians, thousands of unsuspecting brokers and janitors, receptionists and bankers, waiters and visitors in the buildings, and also the doomed passengers on board the planes. The faith of nineteenth-century feminists that women's entrance into the public sphere would rectify and redeem it: what had Anna Julia Cooper believed? I reached up to turn on the overhead light and pulled out my copy of *A Voice from the South:*

> You will not find theology consigning infants to lakes of unquenchable fire long after women have had a chance to grasp, master, and wield its dogmas. . . . you will not find political economists declaring that the only possible adjustment between laborers and capitalists is that of selfishness and rapacity. . . . you will not find the law of love shut out from the affairs of men after the feminine half of the world's truth is completed.

Solicitude, tenderness, devoted caregiving: these were the nurturing attributes Cooper had hoped to liberate by invigorating "the long desired feminine force in the world."

Nor, given the work of psychologists and anthropologists back in the 1970s (one thinks of Nancy Chodorow, for instance, or Sherry Ortner), need such a view be dismissed as sentimental or antiquated. If mothers (who are, after all, usually the pri-

mary caretakers of infants) tend to identify with their daughters (and vice versa), then girls may become more capable of
a reciprocity that facilitates compassion, though I knew from
daughterly experience that a girl's greater intimacy with her
mother could occasion heartache. Indubitably, however, even
the most cherished baby at times feels wracked with pains
caused by hunger, loneliness, cold, or (worst of all) indiges-
tion that might breed anxiety and terror. With men off getting
and spending from nine to five, at what or against whom would
such vitriol be vented, if not the first other (the mother or her
surrogate), and later at the deficiencies of women in general? Perhaps female-centered child care was at the root of the
problem of violence against women: were the misogynists of
the world composed of people who felt laughed at in the cradle,
shamed by their helpless need for a breast, a blanket, a burp?
The very fact of all those leaky bodily fluids—menstrual blood,
amniotic waters, colostrum, milk—might make women seem
closer to nature and thus one rung below men on the ladder
reaching down from the sanctified realm of culture toward the
messy animal kingdom and even below that to base matter.

While the capsule that was the cabin made an unnerving
swoop downward, then steadied, and the "fasten seatbelts"
sign lit up, a printout of an e-mail fell out of the pages of *A
Voice from the South*: letters must be sent, its authors pleaded,
on behalf of "a young Nigerian girl, who has been convicted
in her country to the death penalty, because she became pregnant without having a husband. Such an act is there regarded
as a severe infringement of Islamic fundamentalist law" and
so she would "be placed in a grave, then buried up to her waist,
and finally stoned to death by the inhabitants of her village."

An avenue of hail, then a dull wet sponge extinguished existence outside. Peering into that cloudy sponge, I recalled what I had said to comfort Chloe's friends at a ceremony attended by some of the children she had helped divert during their dreary chemotherapy sessions. As long as you go on living, the best part of her will be preserved, secure from the contagion of the world's stain. But such words evade the hard question: how could one person kill another? And much it grieved my heart to think the imagination too sluggish to conceive what another's life means—the infinite possibilities of an unfurling succession of days and years simply trashed, not to be.

The nullity of the white bands buffeting the plane brought to my mind female feticide and infanticide in China, and the murder (that is what it was) of girls in a burning school in Saudi Arabia, when religious police blocked their rescue because they could not be seen on the street without their abayas. The more I pondered dowry killings in India, sex tourism in Thailand, the age of marriage lowered from eighteen to nine in Iran, the greater my confusion became because we cannot assume and do not find any commonality of problems or solutions transcending all countries and classes, ethnicities and religions. Nor can or should the relatively privileged daughters of parents educated in Western ways simply export their feminism, as if it were a licensed franchise (with a logo, a Web address, a laminated menu) to enfranchise all women everywhere. Instead, we should recall what centuries of dispossession have meant and continue to mean, I felt as I stared at the swollen clouds swirling around the plane. In the past, as women, we had no rights of citizenship and thus were liberated from narrowly construed notions of nation. Ancestral memory could

therefore guide us, guard us to remember that any effort to lay
down one law on all human beings only flattens the tunes of
human nature like a CD player stuck on a mote of dust, trapped
in tinny reiterations. At this late stage of our history, it is one
of the great advantages of being a privileged daughter of parents educated in Western ways that one can pass a human being
in a shalwar kameeze, hijab, tarha, niqab, or chador without
wishing to make a Euro-American of her. "Euro-American":
the very newness of the coinage I had just learned tolled me
back to my sole self.

As had my discomforting lunch with Melissa Carmichael.
For, though we had been allies before she left for her new job
in Manhattan, indeed the charm of our being in league together (inside and outside the classroom, inside and outside the
arcane world of departmental politics) had at times felt over-
powering, Melissa seemed out of sorts, or worse—not merely
rattled and depressed by the horrific events, as I was too; during their aftermath, actually, the only reason I had not postponed this research trip was my urgent need to speak with Melissa about all the grievous hardships that had befallen. And we
had taken some comfort in our intimacy, but at one distressing
moment in our marathon of conversations, she had seemed to
belittle my research, to question my motives. These disparag-
ing words of hers had led to her handing me the key to her library carrel. "Fifth shelf down, to the left," I recalled her telling me. "If where I am coming from remains mystifying," she
had said, "take another look." To my mind, too, her reproach-
ful remarks echoed attacks I had read some years ago, as did
her hurtful jibe about Chloe, but where and by whom I could
not summon up, only that they seemed to jangle in accord with

Melissa's. While I had looked across the booth at her shapely head (the hair geometrically parted into many tight braids caught up and looped together at the nape of her neck), the fine bones of her face and the clarity of her wit stirred my affection, obliging me to feel even worse about what I did not want to become a falling-out. Trepidation about our friendship and a picture missing in the archives of the Schomburg Center for Research in Black Culture made me determine to track down the passages to which Melissa had alluded: perhaps by understanding them I could fill in the gaps in the feminist intellectual lineage I had excavated last spring, for my past and more recent interactions with Melissa had clarified the disgraceful liabilities of its limitations.

Though Melissa and I had team-taught a course on the Beat and Black Arts movements, I needed now to comprehend how the African American counterparts of Wollstonecraft, Fuller, Mill, and Schreiner qualified or extended feminist insights. Of course, before the twentieth century the circumstances of most African American women must have been so hostile to the mental state, the social status needed to write, that anyone interested in their lives and minds would have to go to the singers, the factory workers, the nurses, the athletes, the cooks, the teachers, and (*pace* Alice Walker and Barbara Christian) the quilters and storytellers. But an albeit cursory perusal—not of the novelists and poets, but of the essayists and activists—might prime me to enrich the syllabi of my future courses and also bring back Melissa's exact phrases, which had buzzed beneath the surface of my consciousness in a drone I would have to learn to decipher, I now realized, so I could convey its meaning, if only to myself. For one is, of course, held captive to censure or disapproval only when it is felt to be just, though how that could be—I had been committed to an antiracist perspective from the beginning—eluded me. The purchasing of Anna Julia Cooper's book would jumpstart my efforts to configure a more inclusive feminist intellectual history. As this idea dropped like a billiard ball into a pocket of my mind, a mere slice of color floating below rose up with great speed, broadening into variegated fields of tan, brown, beige, and green. The progress of the plane, which had swooped below the obliterating sponge, acted on the view like binoculars with increasing power, as meandering rivers speckled with dots the size of flies became highways on which cars sped, and children's blocks became houses on farmlands neatly bordered by darker clusters that soon displayed dappled branches. Just inches beside another muddy river that recalled to my mind the melancholy lake adjacent to the campus, apartment complexes and industrial parks appeared where even a yellow jacket or red traffic light could now be discerned. With the help of the archive Melissa had amassed in her study, I would retrace the impact of black feminists, I determined as I prayed there would be no FOD on the runway. And thus confident and inquiring (relieved that no Foreign Object Debris—for those who do not follow crashes on CNN—had incinerated the plane or me), I set out to negotiate the baggage claim, the shuttle bus, the parking garage, the trip home to bed so as to rise up refreshed in search of a more capacious conception of feminism's past.

Venerable in size, if not in grace, the library would provide me an opportunity of shutting out distractions. How were the concepts of sex and gender altered by the writings of African

American women, I asked myself, looking for a study down a dark passageway from my own and the key Melissa had entrusted to me. The leaves were fluttering red to the ground on a chilly day in the middle of the middle of the country, and I invite you to imagine a cramped second-floor carrel with a desk positioned next to a window overlooking a wooded ravine, at the edge of which one dilapidated cat (had it lost its tail in an accident of some sort?) sniffed around a ragged patch of lawn under a sky threatening rain. It seemed as if all the volumes not relocated in ALF (the Auxiliary Library Facility) had been dumped in this cubicle (so as to make room for the computer clusters of the Information Commons on the first floor). From the top to the bottom of two catercorner walls, metal shelves were stuffed with books stacked every which way, even piled up on the floor and high up near the ceiling, leaving very little space to stretch or step about. "Cats don't go to heaven," I found myself humming, "and women can't write the plays of Shakespeare"—that is the sort of talk gentlemen like Matthew Arnold used to pride themselves on, as they shrank the borders of ignorance. Anna Julia Cooper was particularly hilarious about Arnold's astonishment when lecturing in America that the women in his audience "paid as close attention as the men, *all the way through*" and his worry that higher education for women "'—eh—don't you think it—eh—spoils their *chawnces,* you know!'" But what Cooper emphatically did know was that the barriers facing white women paled in comparison to those raised against the "colored women" to whom she had devoted her energies.

What sentences on the page had Melissa's sarcastic allegations evoked, I wondered as I conceded that they could not possibly have come at the beginning of African American women's history, when it would have been inconceivable for black women to argue with Wollstonecraft or Fuller. "Fifth shelf down, to the left," Melissa had said, but I found myself looking at the top shelf and considering how impossible it is to know enough about the early circumstances of black women, to understand how inhibiting they must have been, for the scarcity of facts was an indisputable barrier. What were the sources of strength that led Harriet Tubman to execute the first and only military campaign planned by a woman in the United States? On June 2, 1863, despite grave odds—because of an overseer's wrath, she suffered narcoleptic seizures—she had managed to rescue seven hundred fifty slaves from Confederate forces. Wouldn't this "black Moses" of the Underground Railroad have found somewhat absurd Wollstonecraft's complaint that men "render us alluring objects," who are made "weak" and "dependent" by overprotection? One was stymied from answering such questions by the absence of memoirs or diaries, letters or sufficient collections of anecdotes.

Certain words in the history books (by scholars like Jacqueline Jones and Paula Giddings) seemed especially ominous: "floating coffins" . . . "damaged chattel tossed overboard" . . . "bodies mortgaged, shackled, branded" . . . "reading and writing, marriage and parenting outlawed" . . . "females bred like cattle, males put to stud." Fiery as Harriet Tubman and Sojourner Truth must have been in their advocacy of abolition and women's rights, only today are biographers beginning to excavate information about their families and relations, their birth dates and places, their temperaments—so hampered were they by childbearing, illiteracy, and having always to be doing backbreaking labor they did not want to do, and doing it as slaves. Sojourner Truth's famous oratory in "Ain't I a Woman?" directly addresses these issues, though she may have also been responding to the accusation that she was a man: what thoughts impelled the New York slave Isabella to transform herself into a preacher and singer strong enough to bare her breasts at a suffrage convention and retort that they had suckled not only her own offspring but many white babies, and would her opponents like to suck as well? Sojourner Truth clearly didn't need to be informed by John Stuart Mill that the customs of her country were highly unnatural; was she suggesting that black women had been sexed female (as sources of babies and milk), but not gendered feminine (as fonts of chivalry or respect)? Did the feminization white women lamented look like a sinecure compared to the degendering that accompanied the reduction of human beings to the status of animals?

"Slavery is terrible for men," the author of a once forgotten and now frequently taught slave narrative explained, "but it is far more terrible for women." Right beneath the shelf on which *Incidents in the Life of a Slave Girl* had been lodged were investigations (by Hortense Spillers, Deborah Gray White, and Henry Louis Gates Jr.) into which I had previously dipped and which contributed to my now wondering: might not Harriet Jacobs, hounded horrifically by the perverted obsessions of both her master and her mistress, have grounds to pause, to parse Margaret Fuller's phrase that "there exists in the minds of men a tone of feeling toward women as toward slaves"? Though I hadn't the time to reread the paperback I was holding in my hands, I noted that it was one of the books in the carrel clearly not borrowed from the stacks, a personal copy with the name

Mariequita scribbled on the upper right of the title page. Was Mariequita related to Marita, or perhaps to Melissa? A brief conjecture about that name shuttled me back to the disparity between the pen name Linda Brent and the author Harriet Jacobs. Arresting as I knew her account to be, surely Jacobs could not tell the whole truth about her experiences of herself as sexed or gendered, for she was constrained by "What White Publishers Won't Print" (that was the title of an essay Melissa had assigned in the class we team-taught). Can we really discern Sojourner Truth and Harriet Jacobs or do we only know what editors and publishers made of them, and what of those with no access to editors and publishers—this, too, contemporary scholars asked us to ask.

Perhaps one can catch a glimpse of African American women in the lives of the eminent, whisking away into the background, concealing a grimace or a tear, I surmised, mulling over Mrs. Lincoln's artful dressmaker and back even further to Sally Hemings, tucked away under the south terrace of Monticello, for the ease of Thomas Jefferson's access. Would she have been able to rear her children since Jefferson may have considered them merchandise to be traded or litters to be sold, rather than sons or daughters? What might Sally Hemings have made of Fantomina's chafing against the necessity of maintaining a chaste reputation? When I glanced out the window, I noticed that, down by the lawn littered with those earthy mounds moles make, the curious cat seemed to bristle like a hedgehog at a newfound prey (a mouse? a shrew?). As lascivious as Jefferson may have been with his "octoroons" or "quadroons," he remained convinced about "the preference of the Oran-ootan for the black women over those of his own species."

In stark contrast to Jefferson's theory and practice, the "vile race" we find in early literature seems to be composed—think of Caliban lusting after Miranda—mostly of savage black men in hot pursuit of white women. If severe sun damage counts, one could, of course, include Shakespeare's Cleopatra, who says she is "with Phoebus' amorous pinches black / and wrinkled deep in time," but otherwise there is a blank. While one can envision Judith Shakespeare summoning up the courage to run away from an arranged marriage, I thought as I reflected on the fetters of race and reached for a dog-eared copy of *In Search of Our Mothers' Gardens* on Melissa's desk . . . but at this moment my line of thinking was broken off by a long rectangular Post-It stuck to the paperback's cover. On it, under the capitals **"IM,"** appeared two strings of signs (produced by a marker or felt-tipped pen) that looked something like this:

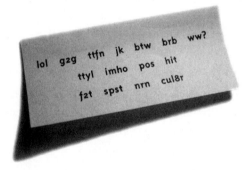

Familiar and yet indecipherable, the letters spelled a foreign language until **"btw"** summoned up the words "by the way," and in a flash I recalled how Melissa had whipped out a little notebook at the dorm dinner that had been so awkward and formal—the students clearly daunted by visiting faculty, despite our efforts to break the ice, until we had stumbled upon the topic of instant messaging, and the tables were instantly turned: they became the teachers, we the baffled novices, with Melissa relishing all the abbreviated phrases she copied down. Her delight, infectious, melted the students' reserve, as had her hilarity at the prospect of trying out IM herself.

But, I chided myself, she hadn't entrusted the key to me for this purpose, so I stopped myself from trying to decode the other bits of "texting," tantalizing though they were, and turned my eyes resolutely toward the third and fourth shelves, devoted to the period from Reconstruction to the Great Migration (there were the anthologies and histories by Mary Helen Washington and Hazel Carby). It was a time when only a very few of the most adamant black women could possibly have expressed their views on sex or gender, for most labored not only daily at domestic or agricultural work in the houses and fields of white people, but nightly at the tasks their own families needed for survival. When the polemicist Ida B. Wells was ordered to give her seat up to a white man, when she was overpowered by other men dragging her to the smoker, didn't the applauding passengers have to have been white women since Wells had been seated in the ladies' car of the Chesapeake and Ohio train? Some thirty years after the birth of Olive Schreiner, a muckraking journalist had determined to risk the destruction of her newspaper and herself—all for the cause of putting an end to lynching, and so she denounced it flatly and effectively as "an excuse to get rid of Negroes who were acquiring wealth and property." Unquestionably, she would have hooted at Schreiner's bemoaning the fact that women's limbs are atrophied by disuse, that they content themselves by giving "small tea-parties" and talking "small scandal." Yes, I grinned, she would have found herself **"lol"**: "laughing out loud."

Still, with Wells, along with Frances E. W. Harper, Mary Church Terrill, and Madam C. J. Walker, we leave behind those enslaved and freed to consider the daughters of those enslaved and freed, the generation that founded and funded the National Association of Colored Women. "Being black" meant to Harper "that every white, including every white working-class woman, can discriminate against you." Not one copy of her first book publication survived, but her subsequent lectures in churches and suffrage societies protested that "the white women all go for sex, letting race occupy a minor position." A comparable determination to make racial as well as sexual concerns central characterized Sarah Breedlove's grit: **"hit"** was encouragement, to "hang in there," I recalled, meditating on the fortitude that boosted Breedlove's rags-to-riches rise out of the cotton fields of Louisiana through the door-to-door marketing of scalp conditioners and shampoos that transformed her into Madam C. J. Walker, millionaire. Because it did not deter Madam Walker that "there is no royal flower-strewn path to success," as she once explained, all women ought to let flowers fall upon her memorial, which is nicely maintained as a theater and office building in the center of Indianapolis, for it was she who established the philanthropic tradition that would eventuate in the phenomenon we have come to call Oprah.

Finally, then, I had reached the early twentieth century. And here I found most of the shelves of the right-side bookcase given up entirely to the works of black people during the period generally dubbed the Harlem Renaissance. But why, I could not help asking, as I ran my eyes over the spines of these books, why were they, with very few exceptions, composed by race men? Booker T. Washington, W. E. B. Du Bois, Marcus

Garvey, George Schuyler, Alain Locke, James Weldon Johnson: who were their female counterparts? What were women
of color doing to promote feminist issues among the Talented
Tenth (did **"ww?"** denote "where are the women?" or "what's
wrong?")? They were definitely active members of that elite
population—as novelists, poets, hostesses, club organizers—
but did they support it (or consciousness-raising among the
just as important Nonce Ninety Percent) by producing treatises and polemics, political platforms and parties, satires and
scholarly anthologies comparable to those of Washington, Du
Bois, Garvey, Schuyler, Locke, or Johnson?

Imponderables that profound indubitably require daw-
dling, I mused, glancing out the window as muffled yelps, more
like a succession of screams, reached me through the glass as
the cat slunk like a fox through the windswept terrain to tor-
ment neither a wounded bird nor a paralyzed shrew, but only
a limp bag blown about on the lawn. Rustling crescendos sent
my eyes toward the ravine where strong gusts of wind blasted
heaps of withered leaves down from the branches, as if winter
were coming in just as quickly as each day darkens into night. A
flash in the air caught in its momentary silver streak the bleak
autumnal scene, accompanied by a growl of thunder. It must
have started to rain, I realized as I remembered I would have
to leave soon for a meeting (yes, of course, **"g2g"** = "got to go")
and then moved my eyes from the deepening gloom back to my
desk where, much to my surprise, a book had fallen open.

On the page before me was a picture of a sinuous woman,
crawling on her hands and knees in a patently theatrical jungle
setting, wearing nothing but a tiny skirt, really just a waistband
to which were affixed what first looked like bananas, but then

turned out to be spikes or tusks. This is ridiculous, I thought as I rebuked myself for staring with such absorption at the gorgeous creature—her cropped hair a cap glossy with pomade, eyes wide open, and a bottom raised up like a banner—when I should have been reading Amy Jacques Garvey, Jessie Fauset, or Marita Bonner. But staring is what I continued to do, for I was struck by her glamour, staged in an ersatz Africa that the performer clearly mocked along with those naive enough to be taken in by a blatantly simulated rendition of primitivism. I imagined her dancing like a bomb abroad, gyrating in the jazzy New World Cabaret alongside the pulsing Zora Neale Hurston, whose blackness comes, as she shakes her assegai, fully aware that this deepening color consists of a veneer of the red, yellow, and blue paints on her skin. And seated around a cluster of small circular tables, Bessie Smith, Mama Day Thornton, Billie Holiday crooning their blues refrains. When the cosmic Zora posed on the steps of the New York Public Library looking as snooty as the lions at its entrance, when Josephine Baker decked herself out part savage, part sophisticate, didn't they produce sexual politics in a different key? They were saying Sis Cat did not want to go to heaven and women could achieve the rank of genius without writing the plays of Shakespeare.

How could I fret that there had been no female Booker T. Washington or W. E. B. Du Bois, given the Hottentot Venus and Topsy, *Gone with the Wind* and Aunt Jemima, Sapphire and *Birth of a Nation, Imitation of Life* and *Blonde Venus?* Better to have been imaginatively insignificant than the grotesque composite that emerges of the maligned black woman, endowed with engorged labia or protruding buttocks as a freak or a huge bosom as a doting mammy; miniaturized into a motorized

pickaninny or cut into the pattern of promiscuity; duly domesticated in uniforms or cursed as an emasculator. Besides
the material circumstances—money has to be made, health will
break down—there was an enormous body of opinion to the effect that nothing could be expected of black women intellectu-
ally. Their minds must have been strained by opposing "you
cannot do this," "you are incapable of doing that," of disprov-
ing or protesting the monstrous lies made up about them. Yes,
women had a Harlem Renaissance, if we take into account the
wonderful writers of the period; but, no, they didn't have the
philosophical and political outpourings we find among the
men, whose international reputations brought them honorary degrees, whereas Zora's graduate training in anthropology
and Lady Day's acclaimed hits did not prevent the former from
declining into abject obscurity, the latter into a ghastly awareness that a gardenia cannot perfume the stench of strange and
rotten fruit. Weirdly, both women suffered the sort of morti-
fication endured by prim and proper Anna Julia Cooper, who
was horrified when an accusation of a sexual liaison with one of
the several children she had fostered resulted in her dismissal
from the principalship of the M Street High School, on which
she had lavished her pedagogic devotion.

But just as I imagined the painful isolation of a woman who
considered her vocation the "education of neglected people,"
I was distracted by a lunacy of light coming from the window,
the brilliance of a day brightening into the yellow-blue wash
of a Mediterranean dawn, and the sight of orange marigolds,
red impatiens, and zinnias of multitudinous hues. It was June
on the Isle of May, I saw, startled by the flowers tugged at their
roots by the flashing golden breezes. A scurry outside—was

the cat out of the bag now, stalking another cat, this one with
a tail?—made me burst out laughing at the glittering sky, at the
difference a tail makes. As if jolted by a sense of exuberance
inspired by the radiant sunshine, I jumped up to stretch toward the "fifth shelf down, to the left," where the books were
jammed in so tightly that, when I removed one, a whole host
of others fell down on the floor. Beyond Melissa's instruction,
what had attracted me toward them was the fact that, like *Incidents in the Life of a Slave Girl*, these were colorful and densely
annotated paperbacks, not boringly bound library tomes.

Was this marginal note Melissa's or Mariequita's (whoever
she was), I wondered as I read the printed text—"the master's
tools will never dismantle the master's house"—and pondered
the owner of the book's rejoinder: "with whose, then?" In another volume, I studied the underlined sentence, "The black
woman's relative independence, emanating from her open
participation in the struggle for existence, has always been
but another dimension of her oppression," which produced
the penciled outburst in caps: "NO SEPARATE SPHERES." In yet
another, a passage was asterisked: "The Americanized black
man's reaction to his inability to earn enough to support his
family, his 'impotence,' his lack of concrete power, was to
vent his resentment on the person in this society who could
do least about it—his woman." Next to this appeared a somewhat defiant though mysterious phrase: "Take that Chodorow
& Co!" As I stirred some of these books around, feeling like
an eavesdropper or spy, "in my humble opinion" (**"imho"**!) it
seemed that Melissa or Mariequita or Marita had clearly been
enlivened to energizing insights into sex, gender, and race not

only by the words of Audre Lorde, Angela Davis, and Michele
Wallace but by a generation of their descendants whose writings on politics, philosophy, psychology, history, and law were
scattered now all over the floor of the carrel.

As I have already said it was an October day, I dare not
imperil my tale by changing the season, but I was myself so
amazed by the marigolds, impatiens, and zinnias that I cracked
the window open a bit and the spirit of those summer breezes
turned the pages of the books strewn around my feet and on
the desk. As if someone had let up a shade, a beam of light
shone directly on a passage Melissa or Mariequita had drawn a
box around and adorned with confirming checkmarks: "White
women who dominate feminist discourse . . . have little or no
understanding of white supremacy as a racial politic, of the
psychological impact of class, of their political status within a
racist, sexist, capitalist state." The words on the page hewed
down great blocks that had always stood there, and the light
coming in was arctic: these were the words that echoed Melissa's accusation that white women have "controlled" feminist
thinking, that they have "neither the requisite comprehension nor the inalienable right" to represent African American
women's interests. Melissa really seemed to believe that feminists like me emphasize the common oppression of women to
promote nothing more than our own selfish interests, our own
exclusionary "bourgeois ideology." Was it true, as she and bell
hooks alleged, that I had "dominated" or silenced her, that I
had perpetuated the subjugation of black women? Here, I felt,
was an awkward break in which my mind swerved toward rancor and pain, a sensation I can only describe as a sort of buck-

ling or balking of my spirit. For, like Melissa, bell hooks wasn't speaking with me or even to me, but about me and in terms that were highly distressing, to say the least.

A clap of thunder, followed by the thud of rain, sounded outside. Fiction must stick to what my mother used to call "true facts," and so it was still a chilly fall morning and those apparitions of colorful petals merely the glistening of orange, red, and yellow leaves dying on wet black boughs. The copy cats were still chasing about, despite a wind strong enough to keep the bag in play above their race around a mole hill that rose like a mountain between them. On the pane, one drop after another slid down, paused, and then slid down again. Perhaps that earlier yellowed light signaled an untimely tornado, the sort that often occurs in spring? Such a conjecture could only serve (during the second it took me to shut the window) as a pretext for delaying the sting of what I took to be an unfair caricature of myself. Though the beeping of my Palm informed me it was time to go, I fancied I could hear the wind sweeping up huge mounds of leaves to pour them as a barrier between me and Melissa until we would be separated by an impenetrable wall, as I continued to brood: how tiresome this assumption that the only ones who could speak *about* black women had to be those speaking *as* black women, this insistence that nonblacks inevitably harbor and recycle racist stereotypes and ideologies. Despite some obtuse appropriations by a few white women who too quickly drew analogies between their own subjection and the humiliations of racial discrimination, surely all the books in Melissa's study attest to the need for all people to attend to the telling injustices of the past.

For wasn't it the case (here I summoned up my earlier

reading of my aunt Mona's book) that the existence of Jewish anti-Semites and black racists and female misogynists discredits identity politics? A politics founded on rigidly defined identities, I thought, relies upon inflexible and simplistic markers of subjectivity, as if people (despite all the mysteries of their complexity) were stuck in some fixed state of being, instead of traversing various stages of becoming. I would not want any woman—even if she were white (like me), an agnostic (like me), an American from the East Coast (like me), middle-aged (like me), single (like me), childless (like me)—to presume to speak for me; nor would I assume she shared my attitudes and interests. As an educator, too, I felt every fiber of my being rebelling against the ghettoization of knowledge, the idea that only certain types of people have a license to learn certain topologies of experience. Political correctness, identity politics: it laid a finger on one's lips so one had to consider always whether what one was about to say was the right thing to say, an effect particularly fatal to the mental freedom one wants for conversations in the classroom; not **"pos"** ("parent over shoulder," presumably monitoring the screen's contents), but **"bbos"** or **"bsos"** ("big brother" or, disconcertingly to my mind at that moment, "black sister over shoulder"). Besides, I reminded myself, doesn't the sectarian jostling between polarized brands of women damage the collectivity feminism seeks to establish? Isn't it true that many white women still suffer economic and social disadvantages, and, more to the point of my own line of speculation, isn't it true, too, that not one woman of any race has ever achieved—or been acknowledged as having achieved—intellectual and creative parity with the greatest male geniuses?

What would have happened, after all, had Marx or Einstein, Von Neumann or Wittgenstein, Picasso or Stravinsky had a wonderfully gifted sister, I asked myself as I stepped carefully outside the circle of books on the floor, locked the study door behind me, and made my way down the hall. What would have happened had Matisse or Heisenberg, Shostakovich or Rawls, Watson or Crick had a brilliantly inventive and ambitious mother or daughter, I persisted as I exhibited the contents of my purse to the attendant at the exit. In some of these cases, I fulminated, pulling the hood of my raincoat over my head, one need not imagine the facts because they are relatively easy to come by. Einstein, for instance, had a sister whose admiration reminds us of, say, Dorothy Wordsworth's dedication to her gifted brother during a life never to eventuate in great achievements of her own. The older woman who so resembled Einstein in gestures and facial expression (when they lived together at 112 Mercer Street) had not pursued much of a career after a youth spent as a pioneer in higher education during the first decade of the twentieth century, when women in Prussia were not granted regular enrollment. Perhaps Maja Einstein was born with a genius for family mediation, not meditation, I conceded, making a dash for the Arts and Humanities Institute. Well, then, consider Mileva Marić, to whom the student Einstein turned when stumped by especially complex mathematical problems.

Numbers stirred Mileva Marić's blood, calculations inspired her imagination, though an absorption with such unwomanly problems may have eventually led her to conceal or even curtail her love of them. No, in her case she must have

known and delighted in her agility with equations, her astonishing inventiveness with algebra and calculus. Her grades were higher than Einstein's; she passed difficult entry exams that he flunked; his articles on the photoelectric effect, Brownian motion, and the theory of relativity were signed Einstein-Marity (this last name the Hungarian version of Marić); but she nevertheless suffered the shame of a congenital hip deformity, the objections of his parents to their marriage, an illegitimate pregnancy, then the loss of that child and the birth of two others in quick succession. It is hardly a matter of surprise, then, that the man who forgot to wear socks in his passion to learn God's thoughts so soon maligned his wife as "the sourest sourpot" to the woman he quickly took as the first of Mileva's subsequent replacements. Having never completed her degree or obtained a professional position, Mileva Marić suffered repeated physical and mental breakdowns, hospitalizations, and the schizophrenia of her younger son, for whom she cared until her death. As for Shostakovich, I was about to continue . . .
But I had arrived at the conference room, and around the long mahogany table strewn with packets of applications and half-eaten sandwiches, a curious assortment of rare types congregated; the meeting to choose next year's fellows at the university's institute had already begun, was well underway. I must have recorded the wrong time in my Palm.

What a singular miscellany of bizarre and obsolete species has been preserved within the asylum of the humanities, I mused while removing my soaked coat and taking the only remaining seat with an unopened box lunch before it. Compared

to policemen and nurses, elementary school teachers and bus
drivers, social workers and mail carriers, did these senior professors believe themselves to share in the serious business of
booting up the world and upgrading systems to run it for another twenty-four hours? Or was such a scruple somehow below or beyond them? Yet the work at hand—awarding fellow-
ships that granted released time for research—was eminently
worth our attention: microbiologists might teach one course a
year, but a two-two or three-two teaching load (of ever larger
classes) meant that artists and humanists often had to cram
their creative or scholarly labors into the summer (since external support—from, for example, the NEH—had decreased
precipitously). On the walls, the heads of past directors of the
board surveyed the scene—some photographed at a podium,
others at their desks—with what I took to be looks of baffle-
ment or alarm, each affixed with a little gold nameplate and the
dates of their reigns. I recognized all my colleagues around the
table and knew from years of experience what insipid cruelty
most were capable of. Since the worst were filled with a passionate intensity, I didn't expect many words from the two I
counted as allies.

The assembly immediately suggested a barnyard or a wild-
life sanctuary. For, gesticulating and swaying, eating and de-
claiming, coughing and wheezing, they resembled animals in
a zoo. Perched at variously contorted angles around the conference table, there was the Giraffe, an historian of the Napole-
onic wars, and there the Turtle, a scholar specializing in medieval mysticism; there was the Duck, the author of several books
on Italian film, and there the Hippopotamus, a Kantian, and
the Lizard, a musicologist devoted to John Cage. I had attend-

ed enough social events to know that for the most part—though hardly the most attractive specimens of their species—they came fully equipped with wives; thus, the joints of their personal and professional lives were nicely oiled and padded. Was this why they were less impatient than I about diddling away their time at pointless meetings? Oddly, as they pontificated more on the inadequacies of each other's candidates than on the capabilities of their own, I seemed to see a bubble form over each of their heads and in it written the words they were actually thinking. Since I suspected that the discussion would change nobody's list and the meeting would eventuate in a simple vote on which of our lucky colleagues would be granted a semester's leave from teaching, it was amusing to compare what was said with what was being thought, or so I determined to do so as not to lose my temper (as I had last year) and devolve into a major funk at the inanities of my peers. For this annual rite always felt unseemly to me, like a fraternity hazing or a sorority rush.

As I unwrapped my sandwich, the Turtle stretched his neck out, plucking it with two nervous fingers three times in quick succession before retracting and hissing as if to himself, "A poet is not an appropriate recipient." The bubble over his head went into explanatory detail: *"Any Tom, Dick, or Harry can scribble verse, but it takes a lengthy education in at least one dead language to be a medievalist."*

Dismay that the ham was stuck to the cheese on the stale bun camouflaged my annoyance at the vigorous quacks of agreement issuing from the Duck, paddling the air with his hands, as if treading water. The one I called the Giraffe, because he appeared to consist entirely of legs, looked fastidiously down his nose (but over the glasses cocked precariously

on its very tip) at a proposal from which he read rather sardonically: "'The war against terrorism is a window of opportunity
to deploy what I would call a Federalist methodology for future
juridical decision-making. By such a methodology, I mean a
method of thought that desiderates human improvement . . .'"

One of my coconspirators, the stiff little Goat sitting next
to me—white goatee, pointed ears, balding head held quite
straight—braced his legs against the floor as he tipped back in
his chair to bolster me with a smile, while the Lizard flicked his
tongue, blinked his leathern eyelids, and popped torn pellets
of his sandwich into his mouth with a rapidity that captured the
disdain he felt either for the author of the Federalist paper or
for the Giraffe who was reading from it.

Meanwhile, a hyper-anglicized accent issued from a newly appointed distinguished professor, who prolonged some
words and cut others short until the overelaborated phrases of
the English language seemed unfit for common purposes. His
clipped, then sonorous purple prose clashed with the fantas-
tically unreal red hair dye that reached almost but not exactly
to the roots of his scalp, making him look like a Muppet. The
refrain forming and reforming within his bubble recorded his
conviction that he *really belonged at Oxford, at Cambridge, or, at
the very least, Harvard or Yale.*

A cumbersome lumbering at the head of the table an-
nounced that our leader, the Hippo, had something to add.
"About the project of a junior colleague in my own department, it grieves me to inform you"—here he yawned wide and
yawned wide again so we could admire the reduplication of his
chins while comparing the yellow of his teeth to the mustard
on his tongue—"that the young woman who distinguishes the
question 'what is the meaning of life?' from 'what is a mean-

ingful life?' has not done her homework. Grotesquely under-theorized!" The bubble stated, "*As long as she neglects to cite me, she'll never get promoted.*"

While the Lizard studied the scales he had drawn on his folder with the attention ordinarily accorded hieroglyphs, the Turtle croaked through his half-extended neck, "Only one of the five from foreign languages can be granted, and it surely must not be the thin, trendy, tendentious 'Imperial English and the Linguistic Genocide of LOTS.'" My only confederate beside the Goat, a William Wegman dog with droopy eyes and a flaccid, heavily lined face, began to rouse himself, but quacks interrupted, as the Duck ceased paddling to exclaim, "The anthropologist who contrasts Geertzian coherence with Bordellian contestation can't tell thick from thin and hasn't read Kymlicka."

At this point, perhaps befuddled by the general cacophony and thus in danger of snagging on the search for a possible rhyme for Kymlicka, I suddenly recalled the meaning of the acronym LOTS. This is how humanists participate in upgrading the world's systems to run into the future day, I thought. Languages Other Than Spanish, the proposal explained, were threatened by rapidly falling enrollments, so we might lose departments of Russian and French, classes in Chinese, Estonian, Hausa, Hebrew, Polish, Portuguese, Swahili, and Twi as well as the overseas programs attached to such instruction. An administration taken with corporate models might fund a few of the languages profitable in world trading, but what of the others? When (probably because of the morning's reading) I recalled reading the LOTS proposal on my trip to the Schomburg, what arose was a realization beyond my usual apprehension of the tired masculinity of menageries limited to full and distinguished professors. Amidst the babble and the bubbles, it dawned on me that, despite their variegations in size and sound, the Giraffe and the Turtle and the Hippo and whatever species I was myself evolving into . . . all of us—including each and every one of the officials hung on the wall—were Euro-Americans. True, as defined by Nordic, Teutonic, or Aryan sociologists hostile to a flood of immigrants, the Irish ancestors of the Goat and the Jewish progenitors of the Wegman Weimaraner may have been off-white a century ago, but their descendants had been considerably blanched.

And the overwhelming number of candidates we were considering were white as well, even whitewashers—the old-fashioned word "pargeters" came to mind. For the majority of subjects proposed as fields of inquiry and the authorities invoked within them seemed bleached of color, glossing it over and concealing its variegated significance. Under the fluorescent ceiling lights, I realized that I had never thought to imagine what it meant that Marx and Einstein, Von Neumann and Wittgenstein, Picasso and Stravinsky were not only men of genius but white men. I hadn't had the mental capacity to consider what the odds were for Matisse and Heisenberg, Shostakovich and Rawls, Watson and Crick to have had (and then to have owned up to having) a brilliantly inventive black mother or daughter, or, for that matter, an ambitious black brother or nephew. Rather than thinking that genius of this scientific, philosophical, or artistic sort has not been and will not be born among laboring, uneducated, disenfranchised people, I was plagued by the limitations of my own capacity to frame the issues properly and so felt too restless to stay the meeting.

Having arrived late, though, I could hardly leave early. I

therefore deployed my youthful training in promoting men's talk without listening to them; in this manner, I could look like I was attending, while thoughts of my own inadequacies kept on rattling around in my head. I might pride myself on an identity-indifferent politics, but white women's gains at my school have far outstripped those of blacks. Besides, how could I possibly be surprised at the whiteness of the institute when segregation rules the social lives of Americans today no less so than it did back at the beginning of the twentieth century? It had been unseasonably warm when I had emerged (the only white person in sight) from the 135th Street station of the number three train, I remembered about my recent extended weekend in Manhattan. In a line for Italian ices, served in pleated paper cups, a beautiful young boy (a child, really) had turned to stare at me; I was startled by two tattooed marks of tears, drawn as if poised to slide down his face, or were they inked by a pen, but for what possible reason? How many of the children at the busy Malcolm X intersection—damaged by the effects of the all-too-obvious poverty, drugs, urban decay, and violence—would drop out during high school so that even the relatively cheap city and community colleges could not admit them?

The world said to such kids with a guffaw, School? What's the good of an education? And how could it be obtained, given overcrowded classes, underpaid teachers, dilapidated buildings, poorly equipped science labs, inadequate textbooks, and nonexistent art studios, libraries, computer setups, musical facilities? Surely the consequences of such discouragement upon the mind can be and have been measured through enrollment statistics during years of the affirmative action measures undertaken by college admissions committees and especially after their legislated elimination. Despite the efforts of diversity officers, the single-digit percentage of black undergraduates at my school does not match the double-digit percentage of black people in the state; a white student has a better chance of graduating than does her African American peer.

That the Schomburg had been a wild goose chase now seemed only fitting. The image I was hunting for—of Zora Neale Hurston with Fannie Hurst by her side—had never surfaced, despite hours spent searching the third-floor archive. And though they had been intimate friends, though they had both used their fiction to imagine cordial interactions between white and black women, the fact that Hurston served as Hurst's chauffeur; the fact that Hurst could get Hurston seated in upstate New York restaurants only by presenting her companion as the African princess Zora: these biographical incidents meant that Melissa's somewhat flippant title for my essay on their relationship—"Driving Miss Fannie"—was all too apt. Could it be that little sustained work on cross-racial friendships or alliances exists because of the paucity or perversion of such bonds, then as now? Or had historians simply repressed interracial relationships—like the affection that existed between Hurston's contemporary Nella Larsen and Carl Van Vechten's wife, Fania Marinoff: didn't they take turns wearing the same designer dress?

Whether or not Melissa resented my derisive cracks about PC, I now admitted, she wanted me to understand that from her perspective it simply meant that finally the time had arrived when "whites have to consider how their words sound to blacks; and since we always had to consider how our words would sound to whites," this only seemed fair: "the leveling

of racial privilege," she called it. Miffed that black intellectuals are always faulted for a divisive identity politics, Melissa
had all but yelled at me, "Who is it that makes me represent
the race?" She had been burnt out by the inordinate demands
made on her by the administration (which put the school's few
black women on every faculty committee and publicity brochure) but also by the neighborhood activism she herself felt
an obligation to undertake. As for her desire for an intellectual
community with a greater proportion of people of color than
one encounters in midwestern college towns—it had obviously
been balked. Was an earlier intimation of this disappointment
the reason why she had taken the new job as a visitorship? In
any case, she had clearly been talking not merely about me but
also to and with me about how exhausted she felt, how demor-
alized she and her husband were by their suspicion that the
people in our community would not have banded together in
outrage and alarm if Chloe had been black, and in terms that
must have been highly distressing to her, to say the least.

As the Duck quacked, as the Muppet ballooned his resume,
the droopy eyes of the Weimaraner gazed at me with touching
canine affection; he must have intuited that the words of every
speaker were sounding distinctly in my ears, while what they
were meaning floated detached somewhere high up near the
ceiling fixtures. Thinking back over my morning's reading in
the impressive collection of the library carrel Melissa had so
graciously let me use, I worried: wasn't it the case that my concern about the impact of race on gender and sex evaporated at
just that point when social conditions enabled African American women to disagree with me? Though I had bristled at being
assigned a monolithic white perspective that obliterated my

sense of myself, had I attributed a monolithic perspective to so-called "black" authors? What about those (like Nella Larsen) neither white nor black, those black *and* white? Besides, how could I—so suspicious about men's stake in or commitment to feminism—not honor Melissa's doubts about my stake in or commitment to her enterprise; and so I worried, had I put in jeopardy what I now felt I most definitely did need (**"bsos"**), for in many ways over the course of past semesters, Melissa had served as my guide. I wanted to believe that my affection had sustained our friendship; yet there, like a body laid up in peat for a century, was that petrified relationship exhumed, but as a dried and shrunk thing. Put otherwise, about the pioneering scholars whose works I had consulted that morning: wasn't it true that they had accumulated materials qualifying not only the descriptive but also the ethical claims of feminism? Begun years ago, my friendship with Melissa—had it petered out in a restaurant booth, when the dead body unearthed from the peat bog had made the pulp go out of our shared past?

There was an acidity or bitterness to feminism, I now sensed, as feeding time in the not-so-peaceable kingdom seemed to be over. Nor did I know how to offset it. Were I to devote myself to the cultural history of black women, would I be in danger of simply blending it into the already existing pot (which would be a loss) or might I be tempted to reserve a separate pan on an adjacent burner (which would also be a loss)? And it came to me amid the sanctuary's animated contorting and cavorting that perhaps it would be just as self-serving to switch the discourse to the back burner of my own whiteness, even though this would at least rescue my pedagogy: in the classroom, had I been aware of the ethnicity or race only of my nonwhite students? How ironic, I thought now, that the first convention of the first wave of the women's movement had originated because of the exclusion of white and black female public speakers from abolitionist platforms. And that the second wave could be said to have sprung from the subordination of black and white women in the civil rights movement of the sixties. Ancestral memory had furnished no guard, no guide at all to protect me from placing myself at the center of the feminist narrative. But being on the margins of that story: what might that mean, if not stalking apart in joyless reverie or, as the texting students put it, **"ttfn"** ("ta-ta for now")?

"Keeping the thing going while things are stirring": a phrase from my morning's reading could help me take stock, I determined, as I also recalled the passages that had so stirred me on the plane. "Courtesy" was what Anna Julia Cooper had called for, and "not the intelligent woman vs. the ignorant woman; nor the white woman vs. the black, the brown, and the red," but instead a feminism "linked with that of every agony that has been dumb—every wrong that needs a voice." The word "courtesy" sounded (to my inner ear) bravely tremulous, coming from a lecturer I knew to have been perplexed by two signs—"FOR LADIES" and "FOR COLORED PEOPLE"—at many of the dilapidated stations of the train stops on her travels.

If I had gone into the Arts and Humanities Institute a woman and would leave it a white (though this last word, used as a noun, still sounded strange to my ears), Cooper's "courtesy" nevertheless caused me to reconsider identity attributes. Such categories, I now believed, were crucial for obtaining a truly democratic politics too often trumped by clichés about race being "only skin deep," but might they someday be understood as more malleable and mutable than most of us have assumed them to be? Whether chosen or imposed, whether a bond as an affiliation or an affliction, whether public or private, probably at most times in a given person's life black and white or male and female take precedence, resulting in a sudden splitting off of consciousness, while perhaps at transitory other times they matter not one iota. I fervently hoped that this sort of salutary cessation of racial and sexual awareness was possible at least momentarily for Anna Julia Cooper, if not when she was traveling, at least while she was fostering her own children and teaching those of others.

As the Kantian Hippo finally yawned an end to the discussion so as to start the voting, I could not agree that the new work on race, which definitely needed to be undertaken in the years to come, meant we had enough lives of Jane Austen or Louisa May Alcott. Neither I nor Melissa (I felt sure) would find it unnecessary to consider again the influence of Charlotte Smith's verse on the poetry of William Wordsworth or of Edith Wharton's fiction on the novels of Henry James. I would mind, and so would she, if the homes and haunts of Charlotte Brontë and Harriet Beecher Stowe were closed to the public for a decade or a century. But just as neither I nor Melissa should be confined to these subjects, it would be wrong to relinquish the literature produced by black women to African American scholars. I knew that, neither savory nor plentiful, the foods we feed women painters and composers, biologists and mathematicians, physicists and political theorists have made it difficult for them to thrive and grow, but this has not been the case in my own field of specialization, twentieth-century literature. So, as the voting began and I turned to my list, glad to see the LOTS proposal at the top, I felt some relief at the thought of leaving the retrograde sciences, social sciences, and the more elite arts, of returning to my earlier investigations into the cheapness of paper and the privacy of composition within the field of letters, which requires neither laboratories nor concert halls, neither masters nor models, neither studios nor institutes, and which has been so inspiring to such a magnificently diverse city of women. Who better to consult than those black, white, and multiracial poets, novelists, and dramatists whose imaginative exertions make fluent all the ethnic and sexual categories with which feminists must contend?

CHAPTER 4

GLOBAL POETICS

THAT WOMEN produced incandescent imaginative literature
in the second half of the twentieth century had no bearing
whatsoever on the prose in blue books I had stacked neatly and
stowed in full view on the coffee table, next to a pot of forced
narcissus, so as to remind myself they could no longer be ignored. Since I hated to interrupt my ongoing investigation into
the impact of feminism, excuses and delays had multiplied until
a vexing day, followed by a fearfully arctic night, put me in need
of a distracting counterirritant, or else the solitary hours would
be spent just listening for the reassuringly rhythmic clicks and
whirrs of the furnace switching its fan back on and off, or for
the less regular, more distressing whines and whelps coming
from the kitchen. As a thin stream of warm air wafted through
the heat registers, I tried to banish my qualms about the irritat-
ing day and the freezing cold by letting the usual suspects from
freshman composition and sophomore surveys parade through
my mind, though whether I found them hilarious or painful
would, I realized, tell me much about my present mood.

What to make of the impediments between my students and the keyboard or the pen? Why did so many obstacles hinder my attempts to teach, my students' efforts to learn the arts and crafts of writing and reading? I assembled the usual assortment of abominations for a sort of perp walk. Introductory sentences bravely declaring, "reality is a major part of most people's lives" or "death is a life-altering experience"; historical expositions on "Magellan circumcising the world in a hundred-foot clipper" and definitions of "a foil as a dastardly villain"; extended analyses of Keats's "famous theory of Negative Culpability," of abolition as "the movement that sought to abolish the ingestation of liquors," of irony "in *Crap's Last Stand.*" It was perplexing to wrestle with critical meditations on "Yeats's use of the sonnet form in 'The Lake Isle of Industry,' which illustrates a final couple following three quadroons"; or exam identifications of the Catskills as "the Congo station in *Heart of Darkness* where Willard confronts Kurtz, with his 'my way, the highway' attitude."

Though they sometimes made me roar with laughter, tonight these near legendary gaffs threatened to conspire with the frigid air and mounds of snow pressing through the cracks around the sills to further numb my brain. Despite the fact that my students spent their semester reading the greatest books by the most renowned authors, there seemed to be no common, coherent sentences ready for their use. Female as well as male student writers appeared to view the architectonics of language from the impassive vantage of a remote, soggy field. The equipment provided on handouts (about mechanics, style, transitions, and paragraphing) seemed as awkward and futile as the wonderfully named tools of ignorance worn by catchers, though these cumbersome contrivances managed to protect baseball players against bruising injuries.

Nor could the blame be put on a lack of tradition since an aesthetic tradition was exactly what I had provided, especially the female undergraduates in my class on post–World War II literature by women. Yet the weight, the pace, the stride of the great authors' minds were too unlike their own for them to lift anything substantial. Do my undergraduates inhabit a postliterate age initiated by an electronic, digital revolution comparable to, but replacing, that of the Gutenberg? Every Labor Day, I stood before one hundred forty-four entering freshmen to proclaim, "if you can see me, I can see you"; I would be hurt, I would then confide (if such a word can be used in the context of so very large a class), should they read the newspaper or fall asleep and therefore I must not be confused with a mirage on a screen. After dealing with my initial fears of facing twenty rows of faces, I relished the theatricality of lecturing, especially in a wired classroom, but, as the term advanced, qualms tended to overwhelm me: about the impossibility of packaging sound bites of wisdom to be deposited like payments on a mortgage; about an enrollment-driven admissions policy that accepted unprepared high school students and then herded them into gigantic first- and second-year required lectures; about overworked, underpaid graduate teaching assistants whose discussion sections often had to be devoted to remedial grammar and syntax, and who often spent more time grading papers than some undergraduates had put into writing them.

No matter how carefully prepared and delivered, did my lectures drop into their minds like meteors from outer space, dissolving into dust upon entry? Perhaps the volumes whose

typefaces and bindings, title pages and appendices so entrance
me seem like nothing so much as mausoleums to them since
they were book-shy, as were the rest of their generation. Had
the older forms of literature set and hardened by the time they
came to writing, and was this why both the young women and
the young men look to video games and movies, photo-maga-
zines and journalism, TV and DVD and computerized anima-
tion, graphic novels and popular music instead of the poetry,
fiction, and drama I assigned? If so, I determined while a series of low-pitched yelps reached my ears from the kitchen, all
the more reason to overcome my personal scruples and vote
for the tenuring of Marta Wheaton, despite the objections of
some of my friends.

While I alphabetized the exams, snatches of the Goat's and
Evie's assessment of Marta—"humorless," "an ideologue," "an
apparatchik"—accorded with my own intuition that her zealous
stance of rectitude would only make her an even more tendentious colleague after the awarding of tenure and the inevitable
(mental as well as physical) thickening that attends middle
age. The few other senior women in my department objected
to Marta Wheaton on different grounds, because her scholarship had nothing whatsoever to do with the established genres
in literary history. But the video games and movies, photo-
magazines and journalism, TV and DVD and computerized
productions, graphic novels and popular music Marta studied were precisely those that entranced our undergraduates,
and what better way to keep English pertinent than by giving
them the critical reading skills that might make them more sophisticated interpreters of their own society's media? Still, it
was odd that someone interested in postcolonial and cultural

studies was so rigid in her dedication to converting students
to an antimisogynist, antiracist, anticlassist program (to which
I myself subscribed), was so very inflexible in her espousals
of it, that I found myself perversely at odds with her. In fun-
damental sympathy with the political agenda she advocated, I
nevertheless felt myself twisted into knots in Marta Wheaton's
presence, agreeing with most of the points she made about institutional policies, but irrationally opposed to the inflexibility
of her manner of making them.

Perhaps it was only a matter of my getting older, I thought
as the pile of blue books in my hands seemed to grow heavier.
With just a decade left before retirement, how much longer
could I expect myself to pencil in corrections to sentences that
committed atrocities beggaring description, even (as in this
case) when composed by junior and senior English majors?
As I started to count the exams because it might be easier to
get myself to read them in smaller groups of, say, five, I pondered the oddity of a job in which the undergraduates shopping
around for courses stayed exactly the same age (around twenty
years old, give or take a few years), while this fact only drama-
tized my own inability to stop the clock. Yet further procras-
tination was impossible, I realized, looking at a row of sharp-
ened number two pencils resting on the green class roster;
I simply had to get the grading done before the end of finals
week, when all but the foreign students would leave town for
the winter break. Although alphabetizing and counting were
obviously diversionary tactics, they did somehow manage to
pique my curiosity about the several students I had found particularly engaging—especially those who had taken this course
for women's studies credit. How did they manage the question

I had put to them on their final exam: had post–World War II women writers solved the problems that perplexed so many of their female predecessors? I wouldn't have to read every sentence, I assured myself. Indeed, it was incumbent upon me *not* to read each sentence, a process that would inevitably lead to minute editing of exams rarely reclaimed by their authors, since I wanted to judge how well those students who had conscientiously attended class dealt with the material, even if they were not the most talented writers in the class. The better writers would be rewarded with higher grades on the two required papers, but even miserable writers sometimes grasped insights and ideas with an acumen I wanted to prize so as to keep them motivated in their future studies. Besides, these blue books were composed under the pressure of a fifty-minute time period, during the fatigue of the term's end, when pens ran out of ink, noses dripped, chests hacked, and an unconscionable number of grandmothers threatened to bite the dust, if (that is) their descendants could not receive an extension or an incomplete.

I shuffled around in the stack until I found the exam of Olivia, whom I still privately called Nimbus, though her halo of curls was brown now, and ran my eye down one page and then the next and the next of handwriting still childish in its large loops and curlicues and circular dots or dashes over the letter "i."

A solid B or at least a B–, it seemed to me, as I heeded the rattling of a chain punctuated by tap-tappings on the kitchen linoleum, for Nimbus had a thesis and lots of evidence, despite an eerie simultaneity to her listings.

Of course, there was the all too common conflation of writer with speaker, the standard inattention to form and chronology,

...saw <u>Vagina Monologues</u> last Valentines Day, totally awesome... Sexton's uterus, Hacker's lesbian love poems, like Nin giving birth to a stillborn and Sharon Olds to a live baby... Edna St. Vincent Millay went out every night looking for sex and not ashamed to say so... not just the happy experiences that women writers ignored before... painful abortions suffered by Gwendolyn Brook's mother... sexual molestation in Flannery O'Connor, Alice Munro, Joyce Carol Oates, and Margaret Atwood... but lots of women chock full of desire and not embarrassed... Angela Carter's Little Red Riding Hood a vicarious carnivore as bad as the Big Bad Wolf... all telling the truth about the body... still, nothing about the differently-abled body so no positive role models here for me... certainly not Helga, poor thing... and the lady masturbating to <u>The Sound of Music</u> (can't remember her name) sounds real old and creeps me out.

P.S. I loved your course ☺☺☺!!!

and I couldn't recall a story about a character "masturbating to" (at? during? while listening to a record or watching a movie of?) *The Sound of Music*. But Nimbus had done her homework, I felt, smiling at her smiley faces as the furnace fan hummed on while higher-pitched yelps de-escalated into moans. She had gotten at something, since abortions and childbearing, private body parts and erotic desires as well as frightening acts of abduction or abuse were often treated more euphemistically by earlier women writers who had to camouflage or hide physical experiences thought to be unladylike or unmentionable. I was touched, too, by the reflection that, despite my repeated attempts to explain why great literature rarely provides positive role models, Nimbus had clearly been searching through the pages of the anthology for a character whose body resembled her own, though I did not know and could not inquire into the reasons why she had to use steel crutches to get around (nor did I remember having seen them last spring in Marita's classroom). Like the perfectly buffed bodies of the boys with six-packs plastered all over bus billboards in Manhattan, like the size-zero dresses in the department stores' window displays, maybe only certain bodies get their share of commercial publicity, aesthetic attention.

Was it because of the fetishized body—youthful, healthy, trim—that my aunt Mona had to deal with her husband's indiscretions with students, now too blatant to be ignored? So as not to sail down that particular stream, I fished out Nell's blue book, composed in a difficult-to-read penciled scrawl.

Impressed with her Latin, I noted that she did, in fact, provide subtle textual interpretations that, along with the quotes (it had not been an open book test!), made me perfectly

... used to be either biological procreativity/or aesthetic creativity... see the historical figures in Top Girls ... no children produced by Austen, Eliot, the Brontës, Dickinson, Rossetti, but also not by Mansfield, Sitwell, Barnes, Moore, Larsen, Hurston, West... now both/and... mother-writers like Levertov and Paley, Erdrich and Angelou, Le Guin and Rita Dove, Maxine Hong Kingston and Hisaye Yamamoto, Bharati Mukherjee and Jamaica Kincaid... mother as especially powerful voice... Lucille Clifton's mama teaches her girls, "first time a white man /opens his fly / like a good thing /we'll just laugh / laugh real loud"... the "unknown bards" Paule Marshall learned from were the ladies in her mother's basement kitchen... but I want to end with readings of maternal artistry in Ama Ata Aidoo and Buchi Emecheta... Requiescat in Pace, Angelus Domini exultant, so I went to pour a glass of wine as a libation to Nell's success. Did the emergence of the mother-writer *necessarily* mean the death of the Angel in the House, I wondered, thinking this might be an excellent senior honors project for Nell to take up, either under my auspices or with Melissa (should she decide to return, as I hoped). Even though I felt it was still "either/or" (as Nell had put it) in Caryl Churchill's final scenes, even though I worried that Nell as she grew older would discover how hard it is even now to live a life of "both/and," in the kitchen I popped a few ice cubes into the warm Chardonnay and was followed back into the living room by the amber-coated part-terrier, part-spaniel whose piteous whimpers might just have expressed confusion at not knowing the rules or rooms at my place (as he did at Evie's).

Anne Bradstreet and Elizabeth Barrett Browning notwithstanding (and I really couldn't remember Larsen's biography, though she wrote brilliantly about childbearing and child rearing; plus, yes, I recalled, West did have a son), Nell's was such a beautifully organized essay that it turned me directly to the next blue book in the pile.

No one but Arthur could have produced this sort of claptrap, I thought as I checked the name on the cover of the exam. I could sense the indignation in which he must have wallowed while he draped his grievances on women writers, much as one hangs a jacket on a hook.

He hadn't answered the question at all, I fumed, but the real problem was the flattening imparted by all the jostling theories imported from every which source and applied indiscriminately to texts drained of their tonal and thematic registers. Didn't the logic swerve from male characters stereotyped

THESIS: WOMEN'S IMAGES OF MALE CHARACTERS
DEMEAN MEN WHOSE "ALTERITY" MAKES THEM
"THE SECOND SEX," WHICH (CONTRA BEAUVOIR) IS
"BORN, NOT MADE"...STEVIE SMITH'S MONSIEUR
POOP WITH HIS FATUOUS AUTHORITY A PROTOTYPE...
STARTING WITH BRONTË'S DOMINEERING MR. ROCHESTER,
ELIOT'S MR. CASAUBON, CHOPIN'S MR. PONTELLIER,
MEN APPEAR AS COMBATIVE "COCKS" (BISHOP),
CUTTING KNIVES (SWENSON), NAZI DADDIES
(PLATH), AND DRUNK ABUSERS (BOLAND)...
THE NAME "MANLY POINTER" POINTS TO A
SUCCESSION OF HYPER-PHALLICIZED RAPISTS
AND PRICKS (SEE BOWEN, MCCULLERS, LESSING,
GORDIMER, OZICK, O'BRIEN)...DESPITE GROSS
EXAGGERATIONS, SHOULDN'T CHALK IT UP TO
WHAT BAKHTIN CALLS "THE CARNIVALESQUE,"
BUT INSTEAD A THROWBACK TO "ESSENTIALISM"
THAT TURNS MEN INTO THE OTHER...FEMALE
CHARACTERS MAY LOSE THE BATTLE OF THE
SEXES, BUT WOMEN AUTHORS ARE THE VICTORS.
THEIR MALE "SUBALTERNS" CAN'T SPEAK!
(PROBABLY I SHOULDN'T EITHER.)

as monsters to male readers as women writers' "subalterns"? In any case, short of trendy phraseology, what does the rank of a subordinate military officer in the Indian army have to do with McCullers's Bible salesman, Ozick's fascist guard, or Lessing's London sophisticate? And did Arthur classify Brontë, Eliot, and Chopin in the post–World War II period? As I marked a "C" on the cover, Pinka—who had sniffed about the corners of the room—lay down by my feet and began what promised to be a veritable anthology of snores to accompany the furnace fan's clicks and whirrs.

While I pondered what I took to be the rather sinister final parentheses in Arthur's answer, it looked to me that even in his sleep Pinka was distressed, judging by the twitching of his wet snout and bedraggled tail, the intermittent rippling of his coat, the licking of his tender foot pads, the jangling of the chain around his neck when he scratched his ears with his paws. As he shifted his position again and again, as his nose trembled and snores threatened to choke into peevish grunts and grunts into slobbering groans, I stroked his head and neck, wondering if I should wake him from what must have been a whirlwind of tumultuous emotion, though surely unlike my own nightmares, which usually devolved from the evening news (anthrax in rural mailboxes, suicide bombings in Jerusalem, Palestinian towns razed), but which sometimes revolved around horrific hieroglyphs—the numbers on a clock ("every six minutes"), a bar graph ("44 percent"). Maybe he missed Evie and the apartment they shared, I speculated, deciding to let sleeping dogs lie (since he had sounded even more miserable in the kitchen), though an upbringing I never could slough off made it incumbent upon me to wash my hands.

Standing before the mirror at the bathroom sink, I let the answering machine take the phone message since I was smarting from Arthur's insinuation that somehow I had censored him or would attempt to do so with my final grade. It was self-serving and self-pitying, the idea that "men suffer too" (that's how Melissa and I had tagged this standard response of male students in women's literature courses), or so I reflected while pursing my lips to somehow draw together all the incompatible features of my face. Even nightly applications of Clinique's Total Turnaround hadn't helped (and no product under the sun could thicken such limp bangs), I fussed, wondering: didn't Arthur's final remark imply that he felt as confined within my classroom as male readers had been by women writers' malevolent misrepresentations? The mirror had the perturbing effect of corroding me like acid by eating away the unessential in its pitiless image (it was warped, with the glaze tarnished at the edges toward the frame). Surely, I could not look as dreadfully lined and empty as I did in its reflection, almost as ghastly as in the dressing rooms of clothing stores. Was it Arthur's odd combination of petulance and dogmatism, his theory-speak, or the sight of myself in the framed mirror that brought back the wall of mirrors I had faced earlier that afternoon when I felt the heavy hand of Marta Wheaton on my arm in the gym? In any case, the heavy hand had fallen, and it was a shock to me, all sweaty at the end of my twenty-five allotted minutes on the treadmill, where I always faced the wall of flashing mirrors without my contacts so I didn't exactly have to see not just my own ungainly body lurching in its painfully inept way but all those others laboring hectically at a standstill on rowing and step machines.

"Can you make the teach-in against the so-called war on terrorism tomorrow?" Marta had asked, looking down at me from her comparative height. We might agree to think the same on this or any other issue, but what she felt and what I felt rarely accorded and often fought in my mind.

I glanced around the room for the spritz bottle to wipe my sweat off the machine, fumbling for a towel to give myself time to consider, but Marta hadn't any small talk to speak of; the several times I had invited her out for lunch or for a cup of tea, she had always managed to manufacture excuses. So now she only paused to add, "Someone's got to explain to these kids that fundamentalists come in Jewish as well as Christian varieties much more toxic than those produced by Islam. Western hegemony in the global economy, Orientalism or neo-imperialism: that's what this war's really about."

"The flag-waving, the homeland security spinning: ghastly," I agreed. "But," I temporized, "what with the terrorists' violence, their veiling of women . . ."

A student was waiting his turn for my machine so we stepped over toward the adjacent mats, on which several people were stretching, others lifting weights.

"Those Afghani women are more enmeshed in the Western gaze now than they ever were by the Eastern veil, which has its own cultural rationales, after all. The Bush administration is just using feminism as a front, of course you know. We need to inform students that there are people who do not think the American invariably right. There are books. There are meetings. Will you join us, tomorrow at ten-ish?"

The impenetrable facade of left-wing righteousness was never more solid. While I explained that I had an appointment to take my ailing mother to her neurologist at around that time, I noted that Marta had exchanged her usual black sports jacket and skin-tight black pants for their analogue in gym clothes; her black polo and biking shorts on a tall, spare frame set off a pale face against thick hair that in bygone times would have been described as her crowning glory: curling down to her waist in Pre-Raphaelite ringlets, various shades of auburn and blond tendrils enhanced a romantic look at odds with the lanky body in black attire. Though I found her incredibly attractive, her sometimes censorious, sometimes aggrieved air of righteous indignation was thoroughly disagreeable. She was untenured, degradingly dependent upon the judgments of senior colleagues she could hardly respect for their investment in belles lettres, their allegiance to a suspect idealism about the classics and the canon. She would probably be turned out of the academy, she must have feared, because she would not pretend that the authorial emissaries of Western Culture-with-a-capitalistic-C bestowed missionary sweetness and light on English professors in their thrall.

At the doorway of the bathroom, Pinka looked up at me from under his eyebrows in such a way (he had all the physical arts bestowed on those without words at their disposal) that it was clear he wanted company. After going to refill my glass of wine, I settled back down in the living room, but though I had determined to continue the grading, thoughts of my earlier assessment of Marta Wheaton's record kept on recurring. Perhaps her hand on my arm in the gym had felt heavy because of a guilty conscience: I had come to the gym directly from the chair's office, where I had been perusing her annual reports, offprints, and teaching evaluations for a document I would have to write and then read aloud at the advisory committee for her annual review. The idea of voting against Marta's upcoming tenure tormented me—the word was not too strong, for I had always supported the younger women not only in my own department but across the various departments and programs in the college. Yet the review process had disconcerted me, I now remembered as the wind seemed to die down outside and Pinka resumed first his position and then his accordion of snores and twitches by my feet. What had so upset me about the articles Marta had submitted in her dossier? Was it the stance she took toward her subject matter, the subject matter itself, or a sense (once again) that I was being attacked (though I was getting quite used to finding myself on the defensive)? The essay on FC/FGM, for instance, began by asking why first-world feminists always couple the third world with practices deemed barbaric or savage, erotically self-destructive or tragically exotic. Because of Western feminists' ethnocentrism, Female Circumcision/Female Genital Mutilation in Mali, Somalia, the Sudan, Egypt, and Kenya—whether clitoridectomy, excision, or infibulation—has been censored, instead of being understood as a religious practice possessing a logic lucid to its adherents. That FC/FGM reflects other societies' views of beauty (no more bizarre than our own), that it functions as an initiation rite ensuring cultural coherence (again, no more bizarre than our own), that its practitioners assume eroticism is not the be-all and end-all of an adult woman's life (unlike our own sex-obsessed citizens): these factors, Marta claimed, had been overlooked, much as have the virtues of privacy, of not-being-on-display, which the veil confers on quite moderate Moslems in many Islamic countries. By protesting FC/FGM, American feminists merely perpetuate a colonial discourse that reifies the barbarism of third-world men and the victimization of third-world women, Marta concluded.

Again I ignored the ringing phone and let the machine take the call, but this time because I was deep in thought about the "ethnocentric cultural imperialism" Western feminists like me were said to perpetuate. Yet just the mention of clitoridectomy, excision, or infibulation—no less the unsanitary procedures, the unanesthetized five-year-olds—made me want to cross my legs as tightly as possible. Inside the chair's office, I had moved the bust of Milton onto a shelf and fanned Marta Wheaton's other publications and conference presentations over the table. Their titles told me little about the texts or contexts under scrutiny: "Transgressing the Borders of the Economy of the Same"; "Diasporic Subjects Sub/Ab/Ob-jected"; "Boutique Hybridity, Trans-National Adoption, and the 'Politics of Location'"; "On the Abolition of a Female Literary Tradition." Given my teaching, I immediately read this last one through from start to finish. In it, inspired by an influential manifesto by Ngũgĩ wa Thiong'o, Taban lo Liyong, and Henry Owuor-Anyumba, Marta argued that the literary productions of first-world women furthered "the discursive and psychological domination of third-world women." Representative texts in Swahili and in French as well as popular oral forms should take precedence over English texts in gender studies programs (especially those in Africa) since the "'aesthetic excellence'" of these English masterpieces actually functions to turn the third world into a mere extension of the first.

There could be no doubting Marta's commitment to making her scholarship politically relevant; but I was immediately struck by a preponderance of sentences devoted to mostly male critics of transnationalism, immigration, travel, tourism, colonialism, and global corporate capitalism, as if Marta considered herself a political scientist or economist. Most of her attention was also taken up by nonprint cultural phenomena (like TV shows, sporting events, celebrities, foreign films, or indigenous cuisines, industries, and costumes), as if she thought herself a sort of folklorist or anthropologist. Legislation and police records, architectural and educational practices were treated with exactly the same respect accorded zines and raps and advertisements or, for that matter, infrequently mentioned novels (for poetry had all but disappeared from purview). Even when creative literary works appeared, they were subordinated to the task of proving a sociological theory. Taken to be entirely subjective or relative, aesthetic judgments (about the beauty, integrity, or formal complexity of a work) were assumed to camouflage ideological values and thus deemed completely beside the point, or worse. For, since artisans of the written word generally come from the more privileged classes, those ideological values underpinning purportedly neutral stylistic features—of tonal patterns, self-reflexive symmetry, and harmony or of irony, structural ambiguity, allusive complexity—were often castigated as retrograde, their authors taken to task for "interpellating" or "imbricating" readers into conservative beliefs or mind-sets.

Why had the discipline of English produced such contempt for the creators of imaginative literature? And how could a person trained in English—albeit at prestigious institutions like Williams and Berkeley—possibly obtain the scope

of knowledge needed to comprehend such diverse cultural productions, and in such far-flung territories, even if she
was born in South Africa and brought up in Uganda? But no, it
wasn't really the subjects, or the male theorists, or the trashing of the aesthetic, or Marta's training that finally clinched it
for me, but the tone. Since I was all alone in the chair's office,
I could luxuriate in letting my hackles rise, though I had not a
clue what in fact hackles were, and their rising was therefore
somewhat impeded by visions of the green triangles my goddaughter enjoyed coloring along the long, arching necks of the
dinosaurs she loved to draw.

There was something all-knowing, supercilious, and in-
explicably resentful about earnest paragraphs that dictated to,
carped, hectored, or derided other thinkers and the few artists
mentioned, especially if they were American. Of course, I instructed myself, most critics have to find something new to say
by debunking what went before; however, Marta Wheaton presented herself as someone who witnessed the Truth and could
now only pity and despise all those who cultivated Western
ways of knowing. Sentences turned into axioms or injunctions
debunking the "complicit homogeneity" of monolithic concepts of gender that "marginalize, stereotype, or totalize indigenous women." The local, not the global; the periphery, not
the center; the creolized, not the homogenized; the colony, not
the metropole: it was apparently incumbent upon feminists to
propound "counterhegemonic subversions" of third-world
"subalternity," of a first-world "messianicity" bred by "trium-
phalist corporate philanthropy." To whom did Marta believe
these portentous directives were addressed? Had self-conceit
made her fall prey to the delusion that policy makers at the

United Nations would be converted by her or her peers' scholarship or that critical analyses of working-class subcultures would somehow unchain the workers of the world? As some anthropologists had in the past, were postcolonial and cultural studies critics engaged only in a very long and insidious tradition of ripping off poorer people's artifacts and rituals, now marketed as academic commodities? More to the point, were the miserable conditions of women factory workers in Malaysia or (for I had not been convinced) the miserable conditions of those girls forced to undergo clitoridectomies and infibulation really the fault of privileged feminist professors or white women writers? But it would be unfair to judge Marta in terms of these scattered leaves, all composed directly after she had received her Ph.D. I needed to look instead and more closely at her book-length monograph because the university now demanded such a volume for a positive tenure decision.

So as not to forget what I had already gleaned, I turned on my laptop and started a file document under Marta's name. At some length, I summarized the several articles I had read, keeping my personal evaluation in the background in order to trace the trajectory of her speculations for colleagues who might not have the time to read through all these pages (because we would have several people under review at the same time). Then, just as I was about to turn to the introduction of her book manuscript, I gaped at a screen lit up in a vivid electric blue and crisscrossed by sinister white letters announcing (over and over again) that all "physical memory" was in the process of "being dumped."

At this moment in my reverie, the scene in the chair's office evaporated; a tingling in my fingers, now numb with cold, brought me back to the eerie silence of winter in my room. The blue books before me quivered; the Remedios Varo print on the wall wobbled; the Indian shawl draped over the upholstery tear on the red velvet couch sagged; and I had the illusion that the white tips of the narcissus in the green glass jar withered on dry, broken stalks. Had the furnace conked out again? Or were the successive frustrations of the day—first the attack on feminists' "epistemic violence" and suddenly all my labors on the computer lost, then the heavy arm descending, and finally feeling at the treadmill like a traitorous hypocrite—simply too much? Or was it the effect of Peter Jennings's report on cabinet and Senate debates over how (not whether) to wage war against Iraq? I am not at all certain what made me mutter aloud a phrase I heard only after it escaped my lips and then only because Pinka jumped up to lick the tears of frustration falling from my eyes. Was it the anomaly of a human being speaking to herself or some urgency of nature that caused the drooping amber ears to flap about my cheeks, the rough tongue to lap the spray? Maybe, cold as it was, he simply had to go out, I decided as I put on boots, a hat, a scarf, a heavy coat, and gloves.

What a shock, what a freak it seemed to me, as I let Pinka pull me by the leash out the door into the sharp night air, where every expelled breath from each of us condensed in vaporous clouds directly in front of our mouths. The colorful sights and sounds of the day had vanished in silence under a downy fleece, for innumerable people had fit innumerable keys into well-fitted locks, and all sane living creatures lay dozing and dreaming—prone, warm, indoors. Ice encasing electrical poles and glittering on the wires overhead explained why even some of the streetlights had been extinguished. Despite the beams of

a near-full moon, the divisions between pavement and road-
way, between house and yard, between lawn and lane had been
expunged in the stone cold night, erased by the softly heaping
piles of snow that hid contours and dissolved borders into in-
determinate masses. All the more reason, according to Pinka,
to sniff out every rise and declivity, to detect under this and
that mound a bush or a fire hydrant, a pothole or a grate, a construction barrier or a fence. The god of snow, if there were such
a god, was thinking, Let it not be restricted to the very wise or
wealthy, but let all intrepid breathing beings—two- and four-
footed—share my mute mystery.

  With Pinka steering the way, led by smells far beyond the
range of the human nose, we crunched amiably along side
streets, trotting down one block of houses only to grope for
quite a few minutes over what turned out to be an overturned
recycling bin at the corner. Attuned to my rising spirits, he zig-
zagged through main streets and back alleys where undulating
flour and sugar made the sifted world look like a vast wedding
cake. "Wild Nights—Wild Nights!" I found myself murmuring,
inebriated by the sting of zero degrees, while I wondered if
the most volpine instincts of his nature scented deer tracks or
rabbits, for he had begun to lurch like a hunting hound across
an impassable intersection through drifts as high as my knees.
He went in and about the grounds of the university, up and
down where the president's house stood resplendent with col-
umns and the powdered orange doughnut—sculpture marked
the entrance to the art museum, where a bronzed statue of the
founder sat holding out one of his hands and the chapel beside
an antique cemetery stood empty, where the bookstore displayed sweatshirts and a slippery wooden bridge led to a con-

fectioner's gazebo, over to the drooping evergreens and bare deciduous trees in the arboretum—his nose vibrating with the aroma beneath the blanket of snow, while I drank in the essence of the campus with the extraordinary pleasure its beauty always gave me at night. But no, he was headed at a gallop for home, I realized while "I started Early—Took my Dog— / And visited the Sea—" sang out from my lips, to the tune of "The Yellow Rose of Texas."

Drawn by the strange stirrings of his recollected bond to Evie, Pinka had found his way directly to her (to his!) apartment building, adjacent to the dorms. We both stood panting across the street from it, peering up toward a lighted window on the third floor. Invisible spectators in the darkness, we waited silently, unobserved on the empty street, looking for a shadow moving across the blinds, but nothing moved, and even expectant Pinka stopped straining against his leash. The light reflecting on a huge load of snow that slipped from a nearby fir branch signaled not simply my friend's return—she might be asleep so we ought not ring the bell—but something more like a mystic sign of triumph not to be extinguished. "I dwell in Possibility—" I recited softly to Pinka, "A fairer House than Prose—" and in his companionable manner, Pinka pricked his ears as if to share my great sense of elation that, regardless of whole schools of critics who discounted the worth of the aesthetic, in fact the poetry had not been denied outlet. Why was the aesthetic being disparaged at just that time in history when women had finally been able to concentrate their uninterrupted energies on its unalloyed expression? For, if it had found expression only in a very few mortal immortals like Emily Dickinson in the nineteenth century, who hid her hand-sewn

fascicles and herself inside her papa's Amherst house, surely the poetry had sprung forcefully and vibrantly in the lines
women published in the twentieth century.

Hadn't even those of my students who struggled with poetry
anxiety clearly enjoyed Millay with her audacious adventuring
("I too beneath your moon, almighty Sex, / Go forth at night-
fall crying like a cat") and Moore with her crusty concessions
to verse-readers ("I, too, dislike it"); Plath with her incendiary rage ("daddy, you bastard, I'm through") and Rich with her
complex pronouns ("We are, I am, you are / by cowardice or
courage / the ones who find our way"); Brooks with her maternal grief ("Abortions will not let you forget. / You remember
the children you got that you did not get") and Olds with her
material brag ("I have done what you wanted to do, Walt Whit-
man")? Not just telling the truth about the body, as Nimbus
saw, but telling it while brimming over with all the complicated yet intense emotions such truth-telling requires. As for the
teaching of such utterances of intense emotions: it allows us
as readers to shed or at least thin the ego, to comprehend not
simply what the poets know but how they feel about what they
know and how they feel about what they don't know and what
cannot be said or only implied; it helps us experience what they
apprehended, intuited, feared, loathed, loved, not as we might
have apprehended or intuited it, not as we might have feared
or loathed or loved, but quite distinctly filtered through their
conscious and unconscious tempos and rhythms, their familiar stresses and alien strains.

Looking at the few uncurtained windows near Evie's, I could
just glimpse a couple talking by a lamp on the left top story,
the flickering of a TV on the ground floor. Here was one room,

and there another. Nimbus and Nell had both felt that contemporary women writers solved the problems of their predecessors, but was it true that literary history had a teleological plot in which authors got better and braver, their characters more perfectly realized, or did they reside on adjacent landings like companionable neighbors? The women writers in my course did not witness their manuscripts burnt by a stepmother who inflicted needlework as a penance; they did not have to slip their writing beneath a blotting pad, if anyone came into the living room, or stop in the middle of a sentence to pare potatoes; nor were they accused of immorality if they embarked on subjects their fathers would never venture to address in their presence. Travel and experience, intercourse and income had been granted to quite a few. But the consequences of the lifting of repressions—this was difficult to determine. What does the passage of decades, of centuries matter, since writing is often a secret transaction, a voice—sometimes stammering, sometimes crooning, sometimes wailing—answering a voice? For, retrograde though my aunt Mona might judge such a formulation, the transaction between a writer and the spirit of her age can be one of infinite complexity, and some of the greatest prose writers in the earlier periods, hadn't they imbued their words with the lyricism we associate with verse and hadn't their delicate circumlocutions brilliantly communicated their baroque circumstances, their "sumptuous destitution"? If the Angel in the House no longer cautioned today's woman writer to be kind and modest and pure, hadn't other invisible censors arisen, tampering with integrity, resulting in deflections or evasions of a different sort?

Was Arthur—when he rehearsed the commonalities of

Brontë, Eliot, Chopin, and contemporary writers—answering my question by refuting a progressive narrative, emphasizing instead how writers of all periods perpetually return to the abiding concerns? As the tufted duvet of goose down between me and the dormitory billowed in the moonlight, it seemed to signify the capacity of the human spirit to overflow the boundaries that separate us each from the other and thus to make unity out of multiplicity, and then to make particularity and variety out of our commonality. And in a rush it came back to me: "Against Coupling" was, of course, the poem Nimbus had in mind, the only one I knew about what the Victorians called "self-abuse" (though they were thinking about men, no doubt); in it, Fleur Adcock sardonically writes "in praise of the solitary act" because the more usually touted "'total experience'" only makes her middle-aged speaker feel "like the lady in Leeds who / had seen *The Sound of Music* eighty-six times."

Indubitably Nimbus, like Arthur, had missed the sheer hilarity, I realized, but just at that instant Pinka unexpectedly jerked forward and almost threw me off my feet, as I caught a glimpse of what he must have just noted, a silhouette gliding, stirring behind the blinds. He barked and strained against the leash, tail wagging and ears flopping and tongue lolling, for all the world in an ecstasy of anticipation that baffled me until I perceived what he must have heeded first, the unclicking of the front door, and then he leaped free from my rein and bounded over to Evie as she dropped to the ground, and amid the rush of emotion and reunion the two melded into each other in a whirlwind of consummation quite grand to behold. With his acute sensitivities, I wondered, had Pinka jumped up to lick my face, had he enlisted me on this midnight pilgrimage, because he had intuited Evie's return, had somehow heard her voice calling him home? There was no time to inquire, what with Evie explaining her jet lag and telling me to listen to my answering machine when I got back to my house. And, almost frozen to the bone, homeward I turned, trying to pick up the thread of my thoughts about Arthur so as to distract myself from the cold and thus reflecting on Manly Pointer and Monsieur Poop, both exceptionally funny characters, and Bishop's "Roosters," a brilliant riff on the cockfights of territorial militarism. Like some of their predecessors (Arthur was right about the commonality of earlier and later portraits of men), twentieth-century women authors, I wanted to remind him, provided that good office sex can discharge for sex—describing a nickel-sized spot at the back of the head that one can never see for oneself. They had laughed, sometimes with malicious satire and sometimes with mirthful comedy, at the vanities—say rather at the peculiarities—of the other sex. If women have profited from the criticism of Juvenal and Strindberg, Rabelais and D. H. Lawrence, Amiri Baraka and Lenny Bruce, why can't men similarly gain from comments that produce a truer picture of man, I wondered as I quickened my pace. The looking-glass shame that so often hurt women in the past—the horror of being reduced to an illusion of someone else's misconception: had male readers been given a sliver, a splinter of this experience by angry women authors? Although rancor at times warped and at other times fortified the integrity of women's creativity, I reasoned, men in the present state of the world are not good judges of their own sex.

Yet just as women had been stung by the barbs of Juvenal and Amiri Baraka, I thought as I rapidly crossed the deserted courthouse square where the lights on a festooned Christmas tree had gone out, it was perfectly clear that Arthur had been hurt by the reflection afforded to him by Swenson and Boland, Lessing and O'Brien. By putting his hurt feelings on display, hadn't Arthur provided a good office to me, I realized while rushing past the Vietnam memorial, for he had made me realize how many women had begun administering a high dose of looking-glass shame: men, previously puffed up and magnified by their own sense of self-importance, now could no longer envision themselves at twice their natural size; did they suffer withdrawal when the cocaine high of their grandiose illusions no longer pumped them up?

With the dexterity and skill of diagnosticians, women dared to irradiate the truth and the figure in the looking-glass had begun to shrink; of course this treatment would be mourned, decried, denounced. How could man go on perfecting smart bombs, cooking the books, stealing from shareholders, bloviating at banquets, if he no longer espied himself at twice the size he really was? It would be inane not to understand the sources of Arthur's discomfort, or to underestimate them. Moreover, it is all very well to say that students should disregard such opinions of themselves. Unfortunately, however, it is precisely young adults who mind most what is said of them. In fact, what sort of creature wouldn't be distressed by this shrinkage in representational stature? Arthur, at least, had not allowed political correctness to censor his reactions, and I owed it to him to raise his grade. Though he knew the rules, he had refused to jump through the hoops in the prescribed manner, and by risking my displeasure he merited some reward.

"Ai, Ai, Professor." The door of Borders was held open, as I walked past, by an aging woman shuffling out in an orange lumber jacket, red sweat pants, a woolen ski cap, and burdened by many heavy plastic bags. With missing teeth and facial features blurred as if rubbed out, she pointed to a prominently placed poster on the door as she stammered to herself and stared suspiciously from left to right and back again.

"Stay warm, Addie," I called out in passing, for I didn't really know if she had a place of her own and thought the well-lit bookstore better than the snowy streets. But with wisps of hair escaping and eyes darting around fearfully, she gibbered to herself and thrust out her hands with their bundles flying, as if to ward off enemies or clear a narrow safety strip for herself as she shivered off. Was it inadequate footwear that made her bound upward every few steps, or was she trying to leap over frozen patches of ice in her path?

The poster at which Addie had been pointing—the same one that had been taped to the windows of most of the other stores—made me flinch because I refused to believe the most recent rumors, that the police were now convinced Chloe had drowned herself, a case of anxiety about upcoming MCATS and high family expectations. Yet at the reception after the memorial, I remembered, quite a few of the older children from the hospital wing on which she worked, wanting to honor her memory, recounted the baroquely plotted puppet shows she would put on—"As the Stomach Churns," they giggled through tears, "The Young and the Chest-less"—to take their minds off the debilitating treatments; and that sort of hilarity made the reports seem like a case of not wanting to know, not wanting to think about the wreckage and waste. Even though I had never met Chloe, even though I was not fully conscious of what her death meant, over the past five months I had been unconsciously absorbing it through Nell's sorrow, through Harry's misery. Had she been allowed to live her life, I felt convinced, she would have played her part with compassion and intelligence. This, too, the poets had mapped in their sometimes surrealistic, sometimes flatly factual atlases of difficult worlds.

Harry had kept me informed of the dead ends in the investigation: the stalker arrested at Stanford for abducting a fifteen-year-old, but denying any involvement in Chloe's disappearance. Shivers seemed to cross the snow, as an uncompromising wind drove flurries of frozen particles across it.

I turned the corner at the moment a shadow of clouds sailed over the moon, while my thoughts returned to Addie, who was a university personage, her father a past president; she furnished sad proof that neither money nor prestige necessarily protects against the emotional strife that can unhinge a mind, unhouse a body. Rumors abounded to account for her perpetual peregrinations around the campus and its environs, for she showed up at the edges of all sorts of readings and lectures, haunting the halls of office buildings, studying the bulletin boards: a step-brother had sexually abused her as a child, it was said; a mother and then a beloved sister had died, just when she was negotiating puberty; and her father—whether from the intense selfishness of his own psychological needs or an inexplicable stinginess about money—had refused to send his exceptionally gifted daughter away for the education she wanted desperately to attain at any school but the one over which he presided. Though no one of these factors or even their constellation ensured madness, all must have contributed to her apprehension and confusion. Why one person stumbles, while another reels under adversity, why yet another triumphs over it: these remain as profound a mystery as creativity itself, I thought, musing less on the separate life of Addie as an individual, more on the common life that is the real life.

Like Addie's hop, the accent falls more than a little differently now, though, I thought, turning another corner and back to the particularity, the peculiarity of the poetry humming in my brain, scraps of which I could recite and also envision: *"ai, ai, ai, ai /* more of a cry than a sigh" (the foreign line italicized, the second in roman and indented). The difficulty of contemporary poetry, I felt, had something to do with living poets' expressing a feeling that is actually being made and torn out of us at the moment. One may not understand at first, though one can remember its lines. It was the mysterious property of words that always returned me to them, I realized as I neared my house, the rhythm keeping up its perpetual beat, swelling and rising and sweeping the mind's contents along circuitous channels. Words made newly strange by their use, but also the alien words, full of echoes, of memories, of associations, which have been out and about on other people's lips, transmuted in their houses, traded in their streets, plowed in their fields for centuries. Anzaldúa's *mestiza* and Paula Gunn Allen's Kochinnenako, Emechta's *chi* and Kincaid's benna: what is their meaning or, for that matter, their syllabic stress or pronunciation? And what of the even more mysterious signs in Marilyn Chin's poem "That Half Is Almost Gone," where she explains that she has forgotten the Chinese character for the word "love," though she vaguely remembers "the radical 'heart,'" which her footnote informs us is literally "the semantic radical" for the word "love," with a slash straight across it. This same footnote describes the "*ai, ai*" that is "more of a cry than a sigh" as "an exclamation homophonous with *ai*/love, punning love with pain."

Chin's words cannot possibly mean to me what they mean to Chinese Americans or to the speakers of Toisan and Cantonese. And yet, because of the polyglot experiences with which they contend, they retain the integrity of the contingent, the circumstantial, the analogous. What abides is the puzzle of strange words, but also the freshness of metaphors that teach the mind to relish the errors and insights of "like" and "like" and "like," to learn "from the juxtaposition of *what is* and *what is not* the case," Anne Carson once explained about how the aesthetic might be ideological but also how its imaginative semblances nevertheless press against or contradict ideology in ways that inspire dissent. Ineluctably elusive and ambiguous, literature—which is not life, but which we often judge as life—deviates from life, defying the numbing abstractions of the theorists, as well as their reductive politics. Majestic skyscrapers fall; even the earth perishes through pollution, but don't words with their infinity of meanings invigorate our apprehension when such disasters threaten to insulate us in the flannel of unreality? Is it the artist's enmity against unreality, her susceptibility to multiple but incongruous actualities that sometimes allows her to endow the real with immediacy or to reconcile opposing entities? To perceive the relation between what seems or maybe is incompatible yet has an affinity, to sense what does and what does not but ought to exist—this perhaps is the poet's abiding task.

These encounters, settings, and perspectives with other people in other places defy my comprehension, repeatedly send me with my students back to the laborious footnotes in small or italicized fonts at the bottom of the page or the end of the volume. Not just when but where makes all the difference, I thought, for I had framed my speculations in temporal terms—asking whether women's literary traditions evolved, devolved, or stayed the same—instead of pondering the new names—Arundhati Roy, Jhumpa Lahiri, Sandra Cisneros, Medbh McGuckian, Tsitsi Dangarembga—evoking foreign lands. Sex, gender, and race, yes; but also place: despite what Marta Wheaton would doubtlessly castigate as Western imperialism, English literature survives (especially today) because it crosses national divides, as commoners and outsiders scattered across the globe make the land of letters their own country. Although the roads, cut by those who went before, remain bumpy and potholed, they lead in multiple directions.

Born in Hong Kong, Marilyn Chin was raised in Portland, lived in Iowa as well as California, and puns on "Ohio" as a Japanese greeting. Trained as a historian and classicist in Canada, Anne Carson writes as Sappho, Stesichorus, the Brontës, and Catherine Deneuve. Masterpieces may be the outcome of many years of thinking, but that thinking is not necessarily thinking from a geographically defined common ground. The mass behind the single voice consists of discordant and dissonant bodies of many different sorts of people in perpetual motion. Given the discouragements always attendant upon the creative process, Chin and Carson most certainly would need to think back through their literary fathers as well as their literary mothers. But what makes English letters different in the late twentieth and early twenty-first centuries, I realized, is the panoply of life in so many different countries, breaking the rhythms, introducing new cadences, widening our lexicons, lighting a torch in those vast chambers where nobody has yet been. The writers of Canada need the readers of Australia and New Zealand, I felt; the readers of Scotland need the writers of South Africa and Alabama, all of whom must be forever engaged in a perpetual exchange. So extended has been the experience of the mass, of the body of people behind the single voice, that explanatory footnotes in the concluding pages of future anthologies would have to be as lengthy as those at the front of the books, which were devoted to the very inception of women's literary efforts in the middle ages.

Chin and Carson, it was true, did not appear in my students' anthology, but they would some day, I suspected. For English and American literature was in the process of transforming itself into world literature in English. And if they are too assimilated, too Western for the likes of Marta Wheaton, there was always Jamaica's national poet, Louise Bennett, whose affection for dialect allowed her to poke fun not only at the British who colonized Jamaica centuries ago, not only at those contemporary citizens of the United Kingdom who fear an influx of dark-skinned immigrants, but also at Jamaicans who (in moving to England) might themselves perpetuate a myth of British superiority:

> What a islan! What a people!
> Man an woman, ole an young
> Jussa pack dem bag an baggage
> An tun history upside dung!

"Upside dung!": a wonderful phrase for reversing the course of imperialism, but also for the dung heap of history that makes it difficult to comprehend which island contains the colonizers, which the colonized.

Louise Bennett would join Chin and Carson in future anthologies—not that Marta Wheaton would care—because she had the audacity to declare to those who accused her of corrupting the English language, "If dat be de case, den dem shoulda call English Language corruption of Norman French an Latin and all dem tarra language what dem seh dat English is derived from." She understood that French and Latin words created the English language, which has mated, too, with Indian and German, Spanish and African expressions, for Mother English has gone and will keep on going a-roving, a-roving fair maid. With poets such as these, so capable of seizing on truths both creative and deeply theoretical, I surmised, we could dispense with the preachings of Marta but also, given the dire evening news, with the even more addictive lures of flag-waving paranoia and jingoism; it was the evening news, after all, that repeatedly put the lie to the idea that the impoverished workers within outsourced manufacturing industries located in, say, the Philippines or Mexico or India inhabit a place that could by any stretch of the imagination be considered post- (as in beyond) colonialism.

At my doorstep and despite my numb toes, I loitered, watching the stars blazing with the fixity of diamonds as they rearranged themselves around the now fully luminous moon. Imbued with Lorna Goodison's faith—"When your sorrow obscures the skies / other women like me will rise"—I was convinced that, if we teach ourselves how to read and interpret, how to preserve and how to amplify the words of emerging authors who come from Zimbabwe as well as Kansas, their voices would topple all the platitudes of cultural studies and postcolonial academics. As I unlocked my front door, several strings of reflection needed to be untwined. First, Nimbus and Nell had something to learn from listening to Arthur, as he had something to learn from them, for the young women's responses had to be challenged (to be made more supple, subtler), while his grievances had to be aired (to become more subtle, suppler) through the sort of intimacy that occurs when mind prints indelibly upon mind. Then, Arthur's grade had to be raised considerably, I understood, because he had something to teach not only Nell and Nimbus but also me; and he suffered, I suspected, from a case of defensive pretentiousness, probably produced by an atmosphere of anti-intellectualism among undergraduates (derisive of his perfectly laudable ambition to learn sophisticated ways to think about his studies). Next, I felt, we are all still learning from the writers how women live, what they feel, who they are, and why they do what they do. And finally I concluded that I would have to locate a furnace repairman, if not immediately, then in the morning. Once inside, though, I relinquished these speculations (as well as my dread of the cheery tones of telemarketers) to follow Evie's directive.

—"Hey, best niece's machine." It was Mona's voice. "Inform her I've told the kids that the husband will soon be my ex, but not theirs. Call me."

—"This is Marita, just to tell you the bad news. You were right not to attend the convention. All I got was the flu, no campus fly-backs. I'll tell you about the interviews when you've got time to see me—I've brought you a gift, to thank you for all your help. Oh, and Melissa is going to phone you; she's dreadfully upset, wants to vent."

—"If you would like to make a call, please hang up, and try again. If you would . . ."

—"Just back, dearest, thanks to Harry's help. Hope Pinka's not too forlorn, but I'll pick him up tomorrow first thing . . . and deliver the latest gossip." I heard Evie sigh. "You'll never guess who was just appointed the new head of gender studies . . . We're in for it now!"

CHAPTER 5

INSTITUTIONALIZATION AND ITS
QUEER DISCONTENTS

"Not chromosomal or genital sex, not bifurcated gender roles, but a whole range of sexual desires and sexual orientations are my focal concerns": I was reading from a written exam that formed the basis of a Ph.D. oral exam I would have to attend in a matter of minutes, but my mind strayed to the student's director. I had to come at last, I knew, to some sort of decision about choosing my life's adventure at a school that continued to pay my wages, though not beneficently or even adequately (when compared to the salaries of friends outside the academy). For institutional formations shape intellectual enterprises, in spite of our habit of judging them separately. And it would be wrong, I felt, to let my antipathy to Marta Wheaton influence the deliberations that would help me decide whether or not to transfer all or part of my faculty line into gender studies. Better instead to consider the benefits of joining a growing program, soon to be a department, that brought to fruition all my previous personal and professional work. Yet, I could not help but wonder, would gender studies break the sequence of women's marginalization in academic inquiry or only replicate the worst of the other disciplines' dubious manners and morals: under Marta's aegis, might it become as prescriptive, censorious, and predictable as she?

Although I should have been reading the exam, I was staring at a photograph of Evie and Melissa with my mother (when she was still in full possession of all of her faculties) on the bulletin board over my desk and worrying: wasn't there considerable friction between the egalitarian aims of feminism and the hierarchical structures of academe? Feminism, after all, has everything to do with striving to achieve better conditions for all women, while professionals (in higher education, as elsewhere) pride themselves on picking and choosing those deemed worthier than others. Salary steps and grades, professorial ranks and undergraduate honors, entrance applications and graduate prizes, named chairs, even office size and placement—all revolve around judgments accorded visible benefits for those at every level of the system, from entering freshmen to emeriti. Fierce competition invariably ensued, battles for preeminence over the fattest paycheck, the corner office, the quickest promotion, the appointed position in national organizations, for an engraved silver plaque set inside an ornamental wooden frame or a seal-emblazoned certificate in an embossed leather case.

As for the financial distinctions, even at my relatively inexpensive university only those students able to pay rising tuition fees could attend; and the higher faculty salaries invariably went to men in business, law, chemistry, biology, and, of course, coaching or administration. Enormous amounts of money were poured into techno-scientific research with apparent commercial, industrial, or medical utility, while within the miserably underpaid humanities, perhaps because of the scarcity of rewards, the institution had an undeniably deleterious effect upon professors who became possessive of particular courses, jealous of infringements on their autonomy or time, and highly combative, vain, and esoteric in their intellectual disputes, determined to sideline teaching and service obligations so as to become the one who had won this or that, who obtained the most wooden-framed plaques or leather-encased certificates, especially because research was the only activity deemed worthy of material rewards or professional renown. Those who could write did and those who couldn't (or whose writings were deemed "second-rate") were considered the drones minding the store, doing the housekeeping, a task disproportionately assigned to women.

It would be a thousand pities, I felt as my eyes wandered to picture postcards of paintings by Vanessa Bell, Georgia O'Keeffe, and Frida Kahlo taped on the wall, if women's institutional innovations would dwindle into replicating traditional careerist practices and values, for if we had come into colleges to transform them, why should we end up pandering to the insularity, parochialism, and elitism of the conventional disciplines? How can we criticize higher education, if we just become part of its business-as-usual—which consists, as it always has, of putting people into classes so as to fix letters after their names, caps on their heads, hoods on their shoulders? Ought not the education we advance emphasize the activism that brought us into being, our efforts to make intellectual work personal and political through our strong sense of community within the academy and our contacts outside it with

various poverty, peace, and justice leagues? Yet when we first
organized women's studies classes back in the early seventies,
I recalled, I was very uncomfortable with the consciousness-
raising going on inside the classroom—"touchy-feely" was
what detractors called it—as if therapy rather than knowledge
was the purpose of our work, though we were hardly trained to
do the former properly. Now that we had developed quite rigorous courses, though, would our scholarship and teaching re-
distribute power so as to improve women's lives or simply gain
those of us who do the publishing and instructing a license to
become the sole purveyors of the (albeit meager) educational
provisions?

While progressive generations of scholars attained their
maturity, with at least a few academic stars in each, I worried as
my gaze moved to postcards of Judy Chicago's and Miriam Sha-
piro's works, had we started to vie for professional portions and
profits (each staking out her own specialized claims)? If we had
begun by segregating women or gender from all the other factors that we knew deserved treatment, did our efforts to right
that wrong lead us to engage in what the historian Joan Wallach
Scott once called a kind of "finger-wagging," a fault-finding in
which feminist K bashes feminist H for her deluded politics or
misinformed theorizing or inadequate historicizing, or for her
previous trashing of feminist G, whose essays were maligned
as "exclusionary" or "totalizing"? What would happen, then,
if we eventually arrived at Q or R—pervasive quarreling and rivalry? Were these caustic polemics a sign of vigorous contes-
tations in a maturing field, an optimistic Scott had asked; or a
symptom of political impotence and rampant careerism, a pes-
simistic Scott had speculated; or, as I at times dreaded, simply

the perseverance of age-old ancestral voices prophesying war. Though I had earlier fussed about an Old Girls' network copying the cronyism of the old Old Boys' network, recently I had begun to fret that feminist networking (which does, after all, help get younger people publications and positions) might be jeopardized by all too stereotypical bickering.

And thus I brooded, would our very success undermine our undertaking? Women's studies on my campus used to have a part-time coordinator (not a hierarchical chair or head) and an enthusiastic cluster of faculty volunteering from traditional departments; but high enrollments had been noted by the dean so now we have a full-time director, imminent departmental status, a change of name, as well as a curriculum, and an admittedly small but full-time core faculty. In earlier times, we had struggled to get the minor through, but now there are major and minor undergraduate programs as well as a graduate certificate, and a Ph.D. in the works. Not just women but heterosexual men and homosexuals of both sexes would be the multiple objects and practitioners of our study. The scope looks grand on paper, but downsizing (as it is called) has limited hiring so drastically throughout the college that most of the large undergraduate lectures, to be cost-effective, have to be staffed by part-time, temporary adjuncts like Marita with inadequate health benefits, no offices, their salaries (like sweatshop piece-workers) a measly flat rate per course. It was, then, the graduate program that really troubled me, and not only because of the exploitation of its laborers. Would gender studies Ph.D. students become dilettantes, insufficiently trained in the rigors of a single discipline (be it religion or biology, political science or economics), proficient only in routinized replications of intellectual maneuvers developed by the various methodologies amalgamated (and thus watered down) in a multidisciplinary venture? Put another way, would the sociology undertaken in gender studies be deemed sociology by professors in departments of sociology? Or would these Ph.D. candidates only be able to glean a hodgepodge of vocabularies and rhetorical rubrics (without their rigorous intellectual rationales and subtleties)?

And wouldn't a graduate student inside a program staffed by faculty not with degrees in gender studies (for such programs are quite new) but with degrees from traditional fields have even more problems than Marita in landing a tenure-track job? This problem absorbed my thoughts, as I focused my eyes on images by Cindy Sherman, Barbara Kruger, and Faith Ringgold, for there couldn't be more than a handful of gender studies jobs each year. But Marita's disappointments at the MLA convention brought to mind my other dissertators in English: shy Keiko, who arrived every summer from Tokyo to use the library, last year reporting that the government had withdrawn funding from state institutions and so comparing the situation to what Margaret Thatcher had done to higher education in England; gracious Sevgi, who had only three more years on her visa to find a position here before she had to return to a country where women were debarred from higher education; self-contained Alison, who gave up on her dissertation because the struggle to earn a living had to take precedence; brave Steve, who felt he had to battle his own inhibitions and his students' prejudices in order not to be closeted in the classroom; determined Becky, whose two sons had delayed but would not deter her final defense; artistic Sarah and Tamara, the first loathing

the intellectual rivalry, the second the social aridity of graduate training: there simply were no single heterosexual men
available, Tamara wailed, "not anywhere in the vicinity of this
Podunk town" and, she would add with rising alarm and eyebrows, at thirty-two her clock was running down.

"Why many cultures have dichotomous gender categories
remains outside my purview," I read, having managed to turn
my eyes back to the examination before me. "However, sexual
dimorphism indubitably contributes to the unfortunate het-
ero-/homo- axis Eve Kosofsky Sedgwick situates at the episte-
mological . . ." But, as that last ellipsis is supposed to indicate,
at this moment I was interrupted by a knock on the door and
the entrance of Bill.

"'You deserve a break today,'" he all but yelled, pulling a
chair up and tilting it backwards as he sat in his characteristic pose—legs stretched out straight in front of him, the chair
tipped back at a perilous 45–degree angle. He had been engaged, I knew, in an annual survey of the publications in his
field for a bibliography commissioned by one of its premier
journals, but his hilarity took me by surprise.

"We've been sold a bill of critical goods that is making me
sick." He added wryly, stiffening his whole frame, "No wonder
we have no cultural capital to speak of."

"Who, me?" I asked, laughing at how stubborn he looked;
indeed, how the very whiskers on his chin bristled, as if annoyed. "Exactly what have I bought?"

"It's all canned. There's 'Plug It In, Plug It In,' for instance: they simply pick a theory (whatever that means), plug
in a text (no matter which one, the more obscure the better),
and switch on the critical engine!" He pulled at the tufts of the

hair on the top of his head in a manner that explained why he was losing so much of it.

"Have you been reading for your bibliography?" I asked, but there was no stopping him now that he had begun. Despite the look of lounging, I suspected that precisely these surges of adrenalin were what made him such an effective lecturer.

"Or, hey, other choices might 'hit the spot.' Like 'Aflac! Aflac!' No one understands a word you say, but Mother Goose sentences propagate critical quacking—quotes from architecture or political economics goose-step through Romanticism, but they would cook the author's goose if evaluated by real architects or political economists."

"Are you doing this extemporaneously, or have you joined NAS?" I wondered aloud, smiling.

"Need to 'Make a Run for the Border'? Find something spicy to say about the canon (too minutely processed, too homogenized)? Try manufactured links, freeze-dried nuggets from other cultures, odd slices of texts or flavor packets from alien fields; get off on juicy erotic anecdotes, or succulent slabs of political grandstanding!—'a little dab'll do you.'"

"Too much television, that's my diagnosis." I laughed again. "It can't all be that bad," I added, "why, Romanticism is one of the most exciting fields in English these days. Think what feminist critics have done. No longer what I learned in school—just the major five, or was it six?" I started counting: "Blake, Wordsworth, Coleridge . . ."

"Ok, 'have it your way'; 'better is better'; 'Add Women Writers and Stir.' But that has been done and will soon be done to death. Which explains why the elderly and the eminent put stock in 'Reach Out and Touch Someone': get up close and personal with Romanticism, with the profession! Phone home about the fabric of our critical lives!" He paused, going on to sound less hyped, more bitter. "The touching tones of auto-biographical criticism just ring changes on another line, the 'Reach Down and Touch Yourself' number."

"Bill!" I tried to sound shocked. "That's ridiculous! Why, some of the best . . . think of their stylistic panache! But not here, please," I pleaded; "I've got to get ready for a Ph.D. oral—one of Marta's students." Glancing at my wristwatch, I added, "Basically now! In a matter of minutes. Did you need something from me, have I forgotten another meeting?" I rose, encouraging him to do the same.

"No, no, just venting," he grinned, getting up. "Maybe the profession needs an *Extreme Makeover;* we've lost our raison d'être, not to mention our undergrad clientele and our reading public." But then, as he put the chair back against the wall and reached for the doorknob, he added more soberly, "I've decided to vote against Marta's tenure next year. I don't want to influence you in any way—we can agree to disagree—but I thought you should know." And with that, he was out, the door shut again.

Was Bill blaming Marta for the ills of his field, I wondered, immediately dismissing the allegation from my mind. For the Goat had used all his stubborn persistence in the past to promote and support the inclusion of women in the academy. Were it not for men his age, I knew, I would have neither this office nor this prospectus on the top of my desk. That he was ready to devote his time to a bibliography (hardly the most glamorous of jobs) spoke volumes about his willingness to sit through interminable meetings about governance procedures so as to make sure fair dealings prevailed. Would he even have a say about Marta's tenure now that she had accepted the chair of gender studies, I began to wonder, but then Bill's "venting" and Marta Wheaton's "chairing" returned my eyes to the picture of Melissa, so distressed when her new chair had made it abundantly clear: she had been hired to serve as a liaison between English and African American studies; she was supposed to devote all her teaching to black literature. With Mona's input, I had phoned Melissa to help her negotiate between departmental demands and her own research agenda, should she decide to stay in New York. At least being a visitor gave her leverage for such negotiations, or so I tried to assure her since her evident distress disturbed me then, as it did now; so I sensibly diverted my attention back to where it should have been all along: to the exam before me, which was meant to serve as the basis for a dissertation on contemporary lesbian films, a subject about which I knew very little. Standing at my desk, I reviewed Myeong-Sook's theoretical argument, which outlined what she believed to be three distinct stages in lesbian criticism.

First, according to Myeong-Sook, the lesbian was imagined as a quintessential woman; then as a quasi-man; but finally she threatened to disappear entirely. Myeong-Sook argued that the initial stage constituted the establishment of lesbian studies; the second, its queering; the third . . . well, that was yet to be seen. How did she delineate her categories, I needed to know, and through the deployment of which thinkers? First came what she called Femme Stage 1. Because women (unlike men) have been allowed to establish affective emotional and physical bonds with other women, Myeong-Sook argued, female couples could view themselves as part of a feminist community that prized other intimate relationships, like those between sisters or best friends. By the nineties, Butch Stage 2 theorists rebelled against such a goody-two-shoes (her word was "sanitized") version of female homosexuality. Why think of lesbianism as if it weren't related to actual sexual behaviors and bodily pleasures? In direct opposition to the woman-identified lesbian, Myeong-Sook showed, Monique Wittig had opted out of the gender binary, leading others to question whether the lesbian ought to be considered a woman at all. The mannish or masculine lesbian actively flaunts her deviance from a straight culture she has no wish to emulate or integrate. If Femme Stage 1 forged links between lesbians and feminists, Butch Stage 2 thinkers created alliances between lesbians and gay men. Myeong-Sook concluded this aspect of her written with the proposition that thinkers from these two groups continue to converse with each other and debate such important issues as gay marriage, with many of the former seeking to gain for lesbians the rights of heterosexuals (thus pro–*gay* marriage) and many of the latter rejecting any legislation that would encourage lesbians to imitate heterosexuals (thus anti–gay *marriage*).

Under Stage 3, or "The Lesbian Outed," Myeong-Sook claimed that the emphasis on what she called "Buggerage" or "The Higher Sodomy" had "outed" lesbians—not in the sense of pushing them "out of the closet" but more in terms of pushing them "out of queer theory" itself. Her evidence here rested not only on theoretical conversations dominated by men and their experiences, but also on the ways in which domesticated (cozy but boring) lesbian plots on cable network shows (like *Queer as Folk*) play second fiddle to stories of "more glamorous, daring, and great-looking gay guys." The rest of her prospectus turned as an anodyne for this marginalization of lesbians to a host of movies (*Desert Hearts, Boys Don't Cry, Go Fish*), television and media stars (Ellen DeGeneres, Martina Navratilova, k.d. lang, Rosie O'Donnell, Lily Tomlin), novels (*Oranges Are Not the Only Fruit, Stone Butch Blues, Don Juan in the Village*), and plays (*Giving Up the Ghost*). Though I was hardly knowledgeable about these materials, this looked like a promising project to me so I packed up to proceed downstairs with high hopes for Myeong-Sook's enterprise.

On my arrival at the ground floor and beside the huge rotating globe, an African teaching assistant was pointing out his country of origin to a cluster of American students. Take that, Marta Wheaton, I grumbled to myself irascibly while I entered a seminar room that had always struck me as an environment hardly propitious for genuine thinking. Amid the barren ugliness of the room—one wall a blackboard, the other three pastel-green concrete block, the flooring cracked linoleum—Nick and Marta had positioned themselves on one side, Izzy on the other of a table long enough to hold a class of about twenty, with an obviously nervous Myeong-Sook beached at its head. Was it the absence of windows or the lowered ceiling that made the room feel so stuffy? Sitting down next to Izzy, I was informed by Marta that our fifth faculty member would probably be late, and their exasperated looks interpreted this perpetual tardiness as clear evidence of his being deadwood. Since Marta would be Myeong-Sook's director, she opened the exam by explaining that Myeong-Sook could begin by qualifying the part of her written exam that would serve as the springboard for her thesis. Or perhaps, Marta added, Myeong-Sook might explain in more detail exactly which thinkers she wanted to engage in each of the three stages of the evolution of lesbian studies.

"Not sex, not gender, but sexuality is my focal concern," Myeong-Sook began in a quavering voice and, oh dear, I worried, had fear made her memorize her written, would she now simply recite all fourteen of its pages by heart? But no, happily, she had decided to fill in the names of the theorists of Femme Stage 1 (Smith-Rosenberg, Zimmerman, Faderman, Vicinus); of Butch Stage 2 (Rubin, Newton, Stimpson, Castle, Halberstam); and of Outed Stage 3 (Edelman, Koestenbaum, Bersani, Garber, Halperin). That the talk was all of theory hardly surprised me, given Myeong-Sook's director, but I was glad when it came to an end with Marta's opening up the questioning to other examiners. Immediately, of course, Nick stepped up to bat in his usual manner; that is, as if grasping hold of an unwieldy ax and determining to hew a path out of an overgrown forest. The analogy came so easily to mind because even at a relatively formal occasion, such as this, Nick wore rumpled blue jeans, an apparently soiled sweatshirt, and a soured expression used to scolding.

"Some attention to scopophilia and narrativity would make the cinematic work more credible. I say the scopic because the birth of psychoanalysis accords with the emergence of cinematographic technologies. If we have Mulvey, and such, alleging that visual pleasure solely serves the purposes of oppressive men gazing at the female image constructed to be looked-at, then we also have de Lauretis, and such, probing the female spectator's double identification as she looks at herself looking."

Myeong-Sook held out under the onslaught by doing a

great deal of nodding, even an odd sort of clucking to accompany what I suspected would simply become another of Nick's monologues. Just as I was wondering for the hundredth time why so many of my colleagues could not bring themselves to ask a real question, Myeong-Sook (refastening the cufflinks on her silk shirt) tried to turn a cluck into a comment, but Nick continued to hack away like an academic Paul Bunyan.

"Despite the Oedipal logic of narrative governed by the incest prohibition, the look of the spectator can shift, as can the intradiegetic look of the characters, and the look of the camera, and such, so voyeurism becomes a pleasure available to lesbian cinematographers and audiences."

Whether or not this was an article he was himself writing, it sounded more like a lecture than a question to me, as it must have to my friend Izzy, whose hands were shaking even more violently than they usually did. I was therefore grateful when Marta intervened to ask Myeong-Sook how she factored psychoanalysis into her three stages.

"Of course," she sighed with some relief. "I see Femme Stage 1 as locating lesbianism with respect to what Freud called the pre-Oedipal, the union and then the mirroring between mother and infant. The positive consequences of this view of lesbianism are the naturalizing of women's desire for women, making all women originally lesbian in their love for the mother. But Butch Stage 2 thinkers demonstrated that this deeroticized lesbian desire. It also played into the homophobic idea that lesbianism is regressive, or narcissistic, an immature stage in eroticism, just a tantalizing interlude before 'the real thing' of heterosexual sex."

"Yes," Izzy interrupted, gloomily, "a *Vorspeise!*"

"Excuse me?" Myeong-Sook widened her eyes in incomprehension.

"German, for 'appetizer,'" he snorted, adjusting his tie. Myeong-Sook nodded. "Stage 1 thinkers romanticized lesbian sexuality as always egalitarian and stereotyped all heterosexuality as oppressive—this led to the so-called sex wars of the eighties. So Butch Stage 2 theorists started to rethink Freud's and Lacan's notion of the penis, the phallus. The mannish or masculine lesbian regains erotic power by virtue of a phantom phallus or by a biologically constructed penis or the acquisition of a dildo. The phenomenon of the drag king is the most striking embodiment of this stage."

"The pro- and con- adversaries in the sex wars had more to do with feminist antipornographers," Marta interjected, but Izzy had been grasping the table's edge to stop his hands from trembling and at this point he interrupted again.

"Since I am here as a representative of that part of the exam pertaining to historical coverage," he growled, "I'd be interested in your views on the cultural history of the femme and the butch." Exceptionally well organized, he looked down through droopy eyes at the index cards on which he had composed his questions.

"Well, in *Stone Butch Blues*," Myeong-Sook began, but Izzy stopped her to ask about the earlier history of the butch so she began again. "I would turn, Professor Abrahamson, to Radclyffe Hall's *Well of Loneliness* and also to Djuna Barnes."

"Good," he nodded so that his jowls quivered, "and what would you say?" He was absolutely dependable with students,

I knew, like a rock, because he had dedicated himself to acting justly, loving mercy, and walking humbly with or without a strong conviction of any higher power.

"Stephen Gordon in *The Well* is the progenitor of the butch, isn't she? With her boy's name and her infatuations with a succession of feminine women? But she is a fictional character, so it might be better to go back to Gertrude Stein, since she called herself a 'man of genius' and the 'husband' of her 'wife,' Alice B. Toklas."

With its heavily lined creases, Izzy's face tended to make him look glum and severe, but he was attempting to beam the sort of agreeable consent that would encourage Myeong-Sook to continue, which she did.

"It is harder to find a lineage for the femme, because she could blend into the female heterosexual population. But the companionate partnerships of nineteenth-century lesbians—some of these figures could be considered femmes. Would this mean we have the same historical trajectory—from femme to butch—in the shift from the nineteenth century to modernism that we have in the first and second stage of lesbian criticism? But," she added, twisting the pearls on her necklace, "I'm not too sure about making this claim."

"It would hardly be fair," Izzy concurred quickly, "to lump all the nineteenth-century women into one category that way, but you are not being tested on the nineteenth century so let's return to butch culture in modernism, shall we? What about the input of the sexologists—Krafft-Ebing, say, or Ellis or Carpenter? Or what about other texts?" Since she looked blank, he added, "*Nightwood,* for instance?"

"My problem with Barnes, and even with Hall, Stein, Natalie Barney, and Renée Vivien," Myeong-Sook explained after an uncomfortable pause, "is their racism and classism. Also their ... their politics were almost fascist—racist and anti-Semitic." "Correct," Marta assented, as I could have predicted she would. She had loosely twined her gorgeous hair into a long plait, but stray tendrils still framed her face.

With a torrent of words, Nick raised his hatchet—"films much superior; modernism's defamiliarization of the 'I,' 'the e-y-e,' and 'the lens'"; "Garbo in *Queen Christina*, H.D. in *Borderline*, Dietrich in *Morocco*, and such"—heaving it down in a splintering roar. But Myeong-Sook was saved from shattering by Izzy, who—despite the drooping curves of his face—was smiling and nodding for all the world like the happiest Wegman Weimaraner ever to grace desk calendar or refrigerator door. He shuffled through his index cards until he pulled one out and placed it on the table (so its vibrations would not call attention to his trembling).

"Interesting, isn't it, the links between fascism and homosexuality in this period. Otto Weininger—who wanted to decriminalize homosexuality and claimed all men and women were fundamentally bisexual—was a virulent misogynist, racist, and anti-Semite!" He read aloud: "'the Jew is more saturated by femininity than the Aryan, to such an extent that the most manly Jew is more feminine than the least manly Aryan'; 'The emancipation of woman is analogous to the emancipation of Jews and negroes. Undoubtedly the principal reason why these people have been treated as slaves and inferiors is to be found in their servile dispositions.'"

Izzy stopped at this point, much to my relief, but not to Myeong-Sook's, who looked rather dazed. To get the conversation back on track, Marta mentioned that Weininger had influenced turn-of-the-century feminists. Perhaps Myeong-Sook would like to discuss their ideas of eugenics, sexuality, and feminism? The sweat beginning to bead on her forehead, breathing audibly, Myeong-Sook determined to forge ahead.

"*Herland* offers a view of sexuality abhorrent in a number of ways," Myeong-Sook started off, fumbling for a tissue. "Parthenogenesis seems like it would solve the inequities of heterosexuality, but actually it serves the purposes of breeding a higher race of ever more pure women. Plus, in 'The Yellow Wallpaper,' many critics have shown that Gilman's loathing of the color yellow reflects her fear and hatred of Asians."

While Izzy was commenting on the fact that Weininger also wanted to abolish sexuality altogether, I could not but be aware of the whiteness of the lesbian tradition Myeong-Sook was excavating. Also, I was feeling rather downcast at seeing Hall, Stein, Barnes, and Gilman dismissed as a bunch of nefarious reactionaries. But I did not want to look like a one-trick pony, a person with a hobby horse, an enthusiast (as it would be put in the eighteenth century); and in any case, I felt that such objections at this point would only take her farther away from her subject, and we had already gotten pretty far afield.

"Myeong-Sook," I began, smiling supportively at her. "Could I perhaps return the conversation back to your written exam? Because I was concerned by the historical parameters of your categories. Weren't there powerful, though underground, butch communities in the fifties, before Stonewall? And when you label Stage 1 'Femme' or Stage 2 'Butch,' don't you obscure the voices of butch women in Stage 1 and femme women in Stage 2? Even the clothing you describe in Stage 1—the flannel and jeans—evokes the dyke or the radical separatist more than the femme. Also," I paused while she wiped her brow, "do these terms occlude a conceptualization of lesbianism outside the heterosexual paradigm?"

Though I thought these were pertinent questions, I was immediately sorry for my words because Myeong-Sook looked so confused—wiping her brow—so stricken that I knew I had to give her a bit of time to get her wits about her. Not wanting to derail her—she had already put in five years toward her degree, and the dissertation would undoubtedly take at least another two—I launched into an anecdote about how powerful strategies of parody and reversal could be. I recalled for my colleagues the old consciousness-raising questionnaires we used to circulate to undergraduates, the one with a list of questions like, "Since a disproportionate number of child molesters are heterosexual, would you trust your child to a heterosexual babysitter?" After Myeong-Sook took a sip from her Diet Coke, though, I returned to my question. "Why must lesbians be imagined either as superwomen or pseudo-men?"

"But I think," Myeong-Sook began, brightening, "that is why Sedgwick's axiom—'People are different from each other'—is so helpful, as is Drucilla Cornell's 'ethical feminism'; she uses the term 'sexuate being' to mean neither a gender nor a sex, but every person's need to orientate themselves to sexuality. If everyone has to lay claim to representing or imagining their own 'sexuate being,'" Myeong-Sook explained, "this right must apply to everyone, however they define themselves. And this is what the substance of my dissertation will take up, don't you see? The plays and films question any notion of a stable lesbian identity by disentangling sexual behaviors (which are multiple) and lifestyles and identifications (also multiple) from bifurcated gender roles and biologically fixed sex categories."

Since this was a moment in which Myeong-Sook seemed launched into the part of her project where she would be much more knowledgeable than her interlocutors, it was especially unfortunate that Oscar chose it for his hurried entrance. Florid and imposing, he flushed brighter than usual, perhaps because he was wearing a raincoat on one of those unusual February days when bright skies and warm temperatures hold out the promise of the early arrival of spring (or was this a case of the dreaded global warming?). As Myeong-Sook went on discussing her project, I recalled how disliked Oscar was for his snide sense of humor, his self-satisfaction at his own erudition, his deeply conservative voting record on tenure and hiring, and a role he often relished playing at departmental meetings, of provocateur or bad boy. So I was relieved that he sat with the air of being a listener not wanting to disrupt the ongoing discussion. He always looked glazed over with the glossy varnish worn by those who take their own authority for granted. But why, given the warmth of his coloring and the room, did he keep his trench coat on, I wondered. It was so stifling—did that clanking mean the heating system was still on?—that I removed my own jacket.

"Experimental film provides me a way to deal with sexual differences among women, whether they define themselves in terms of S-M or bisexuality, heterosexuality or lesbianism," Myeong-Sook was explaining. "Barbara Hammer's, Lizzie

Borden's, and Sheila McLaughlin's movies multiply erotic and identificatory styles by factoring in myths about the female body, interracial dynamics, religious and sexual taboos . . ."

Myeong-Sook talked on with great acumen about films I had never seen or even heard about, while I remained perplexed about Oscar, bundled up so weirdly in his raincoat, since he was ordinarily a spiffy dresser. Obviously she knew the material she wanted to write about and, more important still, she cared deeply about it. A clear pass, from my point of view, as I noted that Myeong-Sook held the same faith in the imagination of the director that I held in that of the author, though to some extent her faulting of earlier lesbian creative efforts smacked of a sort of condescension. For why were contemporary artists presumed to be unimpeded in their envisionings, whereas those further back in time were assumed to be more immured in the cultures that shaped them? When I tuned back in, Myeong-Sook was saying, "The magazine *On Our Backs,* for instance, and the images generated by Fierce Pussy make it impossible to categorize women as either femme or butch or, for that matter, dyke. Like the transgendered, the transsexual, and the intersexed, or the F-to-M's, the ones Gayle Rubin thinks are treated as 'treasonous deserters,' in the GLBT program . . ."

At this point, just as I was deep in thought—wondering if Harry was "transgendered" or "transsexual" and what that difference amounted to—Oscar triumphantly stood up, really shot up, tore open his raincoat, and (much to my shock) leaped to the head of the table, plunking down a pile of multihued leaflets before Myeong-Sook, whose coloring oddly began to replicate his own.

"What do you make of these, then?" Oscar asked with a
leer, bouncing back to his chair and jerking out his little spasm
of a giggle. "Want to pass them around while you engage their
signification?" He smirked widely at one and all around the table, now wrapped only in the blubber of his self-satisfaction.

Amid the deafening silence that ensued, I couldn't imagine
why first Myeong-Sook and then Izzy, Nick, and Marta looked
not so much discomforted as embarrassed until the images were
passed to me: close-ups of enlarged clitorises (is that the plural?) next to a ruler to indicate length, photographs of naked-
breasted women with penises and naked muscular men without
them, advertisements for dildos in every color and shape imaginable. I felt the need to intervene not by engaging the pictures
but by questioning Oscar's motives for bringing them and in the
manner he had, clearly to discombobulate the proceedings. But
I was not the director and needed to accede to Marta's method
of coping with what I took to be an outrage that might sabotage
the exam and completely unhinge an already tense student.

Marta hardly glanced at Oscar as she turned with great
confidence to Myeong-Sook. "We only have a few minutes left
before we will ask you to leave the room, for our decision making," Marta explained, "so perhaps you should use your final
comments to discuss the phenomenon of male-to-female or
female-to-male transsexuality."

With some relief, it seemed to me, Izzy and Nick and I lis-
tened to Myeong-Sook's analysis of the "gender outlaw" Kate
Bornstein's theatrical piece *The Opposite Sex Is Neither*. Although Oscar tried to bring her back to the pictures, Marta ignored him and quickly ushered her out of the room.

"Sorry I was late, but a friend of mine was attending this

workshop by a devotee of Annie Sprinkle and Susie Bright; I had to wait till her FedEx arrived," Oscar started to explain, but Izzy and Nick and Marta had already launched into a spirited conversation about how Myeong-Sook could be instructed by us to revise her conceptualization of a topic sure to produce an innovative thesis. While I agreed, my mind was recalling my goddaughter's crudest terms—"scuzbucket," "slimewad"—for I knew that if Oscar attempted to vote against Myeong-Sook, I would have to protest on the grounds that he had not heard most of her oral. When she reentered the room, the subsequent discussion sounded to my ears like nothing so much as the hum of Muzak when one is put on hold after an interminable menu on an automated dialing system.

It wasn't until I got back to my office, in other words, that I really understood why Oscar's shenanigans had so upset me. I was hardly mollified by the fact that he hadn't presumed to cast a vote because the photographs brandished in this way—at a Ph.D. exam to which he had arrived late, from beneath his raincoat (like contraband), and with a smirk—dirtied them, made them scandalous, freakish, though they were obviously produced with other aims entirely. If Harry had brought in these medical, testimonial, and commercial images, which of course he never would, I would have responded quite differently, I knew. For Harry—who represented his "sexuate being" as highly circumspect (at least in his interactions with me)— proved the truth of Myeong-Sook's project. Indeed, Harry seemed far less invested in formulating his "sexuate being," far more passionately involved in the new role he anticipated— of becoming honorary uncle or older brother to the baby Evie was trying to adopt.

Context is all, and Oscar's titillation at the pictures and at the prospect of their shock value clarified for me the vulnerability of sexuality studies in the academy, a vulnerability that mimicked (I felt) the perilous insecurity of homosexuals in a society at the ready to tarnish their lives. What was Bill's phrase? "Getting off on juicy erotic anecdotes"? It was worthwhile considering, I reflected about Oscar's voyeurism, who brings sexuality into the classroom, the curriculum, how it is done, with which framing devices, and I would need to ponder the Goat's cautionary viewpoint in days to come. The struggles for insurance, for health benefits, for hospital visitation rights, even for the right to display affection openly without being stared at, the mockery, the petty humiliations: contemplating these, I now understood that Oscar had infuriated me because he had brought to mind the summons, the order to attend the court, the counsel for the prosecution bustling in with a little bow, privacy lurched into lurid tabloids, the verdict—a lesbian mother debarred from legal custody of her own child—the obscenity of a young person strung up to die on a fence in Wyoming, the flames rising.

"When you have a minute, I'd like to discuss that shotdown LOTS proposal." Marta Wheaton was standing in the hall, just outside my door, so I rose to join her. "I've encouraged its author to resubmit; maybe we can help him strengthen it for next year's round?" After I vigorously nodded in agreement and promised to e-mail some suggested revisions, Marta added, "Quite right to interrogate the unfortunate heuristics of Myeong-Sook's taxonomy."

"She did very well," I congratulated Marta. "But what to make of Oscar!" And here I looked up at Marta with a grimace, wishing (for the umpteenth time) that I weren't so short.

"Par for the course," she agreed with a dismissive shrug that encouraged me to focus on matters more important than a reprobate beneath contempt. So I took in a breath and determined to air my only real objection to Myeong-Sook's approach, since Marta's direction would shape its future evolution.

"Marta," I said, "I've got to run—a bunch of errands, and then Mona's expecting me for an elaborate Indian dinner (she's been cooking for days)—but at some point I would like to ask you, don't you think that Hall, Stein, Gilman, and Barnes have something to add to Myeong-Sook's project, that they ought not just be typecast as reactionaries or fascists, even though their politics were obviously suspect by our lights?"

She pushed a straying curl back behind her ear. "Of course, that was what would have bothered the likes of you," her frown might as well have said. "I've given her a reading list—Marilyn Frye, Barbara Smith, Barbara Johnson, Biddy Martin, Minnie Bruce Pratt, Elizabeth Spelman—since she obviously hasn't figured out how to deal with the whiteness of her archive. It would help too," she added, "if she minded Izzy—she needs to acquaint herself with non-English, non-American, and especially medical sources, not to mention the scholarship of people like Lisa Lowe, Chandra Mohanty, Rey Chow, et cetera, et cetera, et cetera . . ."

I went to jot down the names I didn't know, and then added (with what I hoped would not be transparency), "But why do our students feel so supercilious about women's literary achievements in the past?"

"I've often argued that the first generation of feminist critics overly identified with women artists, idealized them as perfected paragons." And just as I was feeling myself an old fogy, addled and decrepit, she added, "But their successors disidentified so completely that those same women artists dwindled into the obverse, monitory or cautionary miscreants." With that, in the businesslike way she always maintained, Marta buttoned her black jacket and strode down toward the faculty mailboxes, leaving me oddly elated, though usually I embark on trips to the bank, the drugstore, and the post office with a profound sense of tedium.

For I was relieved not only that Marta had found a way of addressing a colorblindness I had been unable to rectify in Myeong-Sook's oral but also that she had clarified a phenomenon I had found infinitely perplexing. Whether or not the finger wagging of feminist critics was an offshoot of professional jockeying, her remarks made sense: if the first generation of feminist critics believed they were excavating a female tradition they cherished, maybe postcolonial and cultural studies scholars had to distinguish themselves by vilifying or at least confronting the limitations of that past. But this meant that the age groups coming into maturity tomorrow or next year might just do away with such patently inadequate historical projections, which (I admitted, if only to myself) I had certainly also been guilty of. Marta was very smart, I thought while considering how wrong it was of the dean to foist the responsibilities of chairing upon her before the tenure decision, because how could she possibly do the requisite publishing, if all her energies were taken up with administration—and also with the burden of directing so many Ph.D. dissertations—especially at the present moment, when publishing houses were cutting down on their lists of criticism (which was not selling)? Despite the censorious proselytizing at which I bristled, or perhaps because of it, Marta had handled the oral—and Oscar's outrageous behavior—better than I could have, I had to concede.

And that Marta had included a creative writer—a poet!—in the cluster of names she had suggested to Myeong-Sook exhilarated me, for if the creativity of the poets provides critical or even theoretical insights, as I firmly believed (and Marta apparently did too), then surely the critical and theoretical work of postcolonial and cultural studies scholars has an aesthetic dimension. And so I wondered, were it not for the exertions of teachers like Marta, would I have ever learned about the existence of Tsitsi Dangarembga and Louise Bennett; would I have felt the need to read them, or known how to? Who, if not postcolonialists, had brought nation into the mix of gender, sex, and race? And who, if not cultural studies critics, had brought class, age, ethnicity, religion, and a myriad of other social circumstances into that mix? Without knowing the conditions out of which novels and poems originated, I speculated, how could they possibly resonate with the traditions that indubitably shaped their authors' lives and designs? For poets do not only converse with other poets or confine their views to other poems; indeed, sometimes they find themselves more fully engaged with cuisines, rock concerts, movies, celebrities, and medical procedures.

But there were other twitches pulling at the edges of my mind as well, as I packed up to leave. Even if I value the formalism of literature's engagement with language, I reflected, hadn't the exclusion of women writers from the canon of Great Books (always in pushy capital letters) told me that so-called neutral aesthetic criteria could be biased, rating works about the hunting of a whale or rafting on a river over those about courtship and child rearing? For I had begun my own work with the conviction that male critics had unfairly deemed works about war and sports "important," books about housekeep-

ing "trivial." Also, although I may cherish the Great Books by
the Great Authors (more capital letters), hadn't Melissa taught
me that the histories of women with no access to the education that publishing requires can best be studied through non-
literary sources? On a less high-minded level too, I knew, my
own students need to acquire reading and writing skills to cope
with the barrage of texts (and texting) that increasingly papers
and screens all of our lives.

Mulling over Marta's belief that our reading ought to relate
us to what seems entirely remote or foreign—and only at this
minute did it dawn on me that we were allies in our advocacy of
LOTS—I considered the bolts on doors and locks on windows
that ensure privacy, but also the routers and wires, the waves
of sound and sight that pour through walls and roofs, speaking
of battles and strikes, weather and want all around the world,
the wireless electronic communications too, breaking into
each consciousness with its resulting discords and incongrui-
ties. There is a flexibility and scope in postcolonial and cultural studies which is salutary, I thought, for these thinkers keep
pace with the rapidity of these novel changes in people's relations to each other. By enlarging the canon beyond first-world
countries and high-cultural forms, feminists in postcolonial
and cultural studies teach us how as well as why we need to
study contexts that should be comprehended precisely because
they are not our own. Didn't their investigations into post- (as
in beyond but still enmeshed within) colonialism clarify the
conditions of many people still contending with the continuing consequences of imperial violence? New research on these
subjects would issue in all sorts of innovative courses for undergraduates in the future, transforming our understanding of
the humanities completely.

All the infinitely obscure lives and arts remain to be recorded by postcolonial and cultural studies scholars, I granted Marta. And I tried to go on in thought around this globe full of figures, through the streets of Havana and Calcutta, Beijing and Port-au-Prince, the bare plains around Kigali, feeling the blanketing of my condition, my inability to imagine the accumulation of unrecorded life, whether from the women at the street corners with their arms akimbo, and the rings on their arms, or from the old crones standing naked-legged in the stream to beat linen on stones, or from drifting working girls whose faces, like rays of sunlight through clouds, signal the flickerings of dawn or twilight. Looked at from their point of view, Western feminists, I understood now, were nothing but another type of profiteer who snatched money and status from those possibly rating these things of little worth, and who could think of nothing better to do than to build opportunities for people already endowed with a great deal more than their share. Imbued with values and languages incomprehensible to me, the stalls and stores in Albania and Armenia, the marketplaces of Parma and Jakarta, of Seoul and São Paulo, Hebron and Lagos, Lutsk and Yazd sold foods and spices I had never eaten, never would taste. There, I hoped, the floating seeds of an indigenous feminism were spawning and spreading to issue eventually in unforeseeable formations, unfathomable to me, which (I wanted to believe) would surely help make sense of the lives of the women who created and nurtured a newly international feminism.

Although I sympathized with Melissa's fears that an emphasis on the issues of third-world women would once again eclipse those of African Americans, there was no reason to defend only English-language poets or novelists, I granted Marta

Wheaton, suspecting that I had been programmed by nothing more than my own miserable monolinguism or my own disciplinary or geographical prejudices, for wasn't it the case that American women constitute only something like 2 percent of the world's population? Since literature is common ground, not cut up into warring nations, writers can and do trespass freely, fearlessly finding their own way; and readers sense their minds threaded together with authors composing in many different tongues. Global English notwithstanding, literature departments would have to abandon their linguistic confines, would become highly comparative to translate the international conversations that twenty-first- and twenty-second-century cultures were fast becoming. And weren't those conversations crucial to the survival of the species? The deaths of American soldiers after the president declared the Iraqi War over and won, the sufferings of the Iraqi people—without law and order, food and fuel, dazed by ongoing violence from within and without—and the escalating suffering throughout the globe in the midst of widespread fear of terrorizing "weapons of mass destruction" (as well as lies about them): the only hope, fragile though it was, had to reside in better and more communication, founded on exactly the sort of respectful learning that the most and the least prestigious programs in higher education foster. Yet if not just the well-endowed, elite institutions were to survive, state legislators and taxpayers would have to be taught why they should support the humanities programs at their public universities and colleges, but how?

As I started to follow in Marta Wheaton's steps down the hall to the secretaries, it struck me that I needed to make my decision on her tenure next fall not on the basis of any personal aversion to her temperament or mannerisms, but on an honest assessment of her work, for there was every reason to believe that gender studies in African countries should emphasize Swahili or French and oral forms, though the logic on genital mutilation still seemed flawed. Yet her larger point in that essay—that I don't comprehend such practices—was indubitably true, and certainly genital mutilation has to be understood as a crucial subject of inquiry, even though its investigation places literature at the margins of this newly emerging discipline of gender studies. I felt relieved that after the semester ended and Mona returned to her home institution, I would have the summer to evaluate, with an altered mind, Marta's materials for the tenure discussion that would occur in the fall.

Literary critics like me may play a less decisive role in gender studies than we had at the inception of women's studies, I realized, but Myeong-Sook's exam had proven that faculty in English departments—as in other humanities departments—have also begun to multiply their objects and methods of investigation. If the words of lumberjack Nick rang strangely in my ears, wasn't that because his scholarship derived from film studies? And if Izzy sometimes introduced startling perspectives, wasn't that because his work dovetailed with that of Jewish studies scholars? Whereas gender studies might look dilettantish today, surely at the end of the nineteenth century English must have seemed amateurish to classicists and philologists. Given Bill's advertising campaign against the canned criticism in English, why should I judge the interdisciplinarity of gender studies so harshly? Though I could hardly untangle the cockamamie logic of my determination, I decided then and there: all the better if sociologists in the sociology department don't recognize as sociology the sociology done in gender studies. Gender studies' becoming a discipline (and thus a legitimate professional venue) might, I concluded, safeguard multidisciplinary work on gender, sex, and sexuality from the budgetary axes that keep on hacking away at centers, programs, and institutes. Its becoming a discipline (and thus a legitimate professional venue) will, I decided, enable gender studies scholars to advance new intellectual questions, answers, and venues, quite distinct from those posed by sociologists.

Once inside the English department office, I was struck by the fact that the secretaries had neatly organized the mass of papers students had jammed into my mailbox (they would have to be graded that weekend), even though I hadn't asked them to do so. It was a far cry from the old days, when they had treated me with some contempt—perhaps because the faculty they were used to serving then was overwhelmingly male, perhaps because I was quite young, perhaps because of some inadvertent breach of etiquette on my own part, perhaps because the clerical staff was so poorly paid. In any case, one of the worst moments in this office in those days was not with a secretary but with a senior professor—yes, of course, it was Professor Stevens, then on the brink of retirement, but perpetually deferring it—who, after one hurried look at me, handed me a stencil to type. He had assumed that any woman in this space was there to serve him as a secretary. I recalled my sense of embarrassment for him back then, as I now stuffed the folders in my briefcase to make my way out of the building, to the parking garage, where I then realized that I could no longer remember where I had parked my car.

So it was under the shadow of this complex concrete structure of crisscrossing levels of parked vehicles, where sparrows and cardinals hunted crumbs, that I found myself wandering, as worries about my mother's fate becoming my own mixed with memories of those difficult days upon my arrival at this school, twenty-five years ago. Walking up and down the rows of silver and black, white and blue cars, station wagons, minivans, and SUVs, I thought first of my mother—well into her eighties now, she would look vague or distressed if one asked her where she had been, what she had done, or who she recalled—and then of the group I encountered upon my arrival at this, my first and only job, an assemblage I called "the wives"; not because of any contempt on my part for housekeepers and spouses, but because this highly accomplished and educated group of women welcomed me into their community with varying degrees of envy and sympathy, hostility and admiration.

Most tragically, I recalled, stepping down the ramp on level three, there was quirky Anne, the Goat's wife, a Ph.D. in English blocked from teaching in his department by nepotism rules: though she tried to sustain her research through independent scholarship, the pangs of renounced ambitions and of being a hostess for a dedicated administrator led first to a drinking problem, then to a drinking-related accident and untimely death. Disturbing, too, were sensitive and smart Cynthia, Trish, and Mari, also Ph.D.'s and also unemployed, who dedicated themselves to child rearing with varying degrees of intellectual loneliness until, their children grown, they settled for work decidedly beneath their capacities. Then there was feisty Sybil, an unhired expert in East Asian studies, who channeled her energies first into a hardware store in town and later a succession of lively political campaigns. Despite

this last success story (as well as the dinner parties and teas
"the wives" had sponsored, the convivial socializing we often
miss in these more harried times), the wasted talent, the anguish, the awkward social negotiations haunted me.

And then the handful of women hired during my six years
as an assistant professor, my so-called cohort: not one of them
had remained to prosper, I remembered while moving further down to level two where the overhead beams made me feel
claustrophobic. Each arrived with or quickly acquired horror
stories: of a dissertation advisor who patiently explained that
her pregnancy meant she would never get an academic job;
of a chair who proposed that she relinquish her professional
ambitions so as to support her husband's; of a husband hor-
ribly hurt because the university refused to hire him so he took
out his frustrations by filing for alimony; of a male colleague
whose sexual overtures were advanced under the sleazy cover
of mentoring.

Most upsetting was Lorie, a recluse whose eating disorder
led to a complete physical breakdown. Disturbing, too, were
attractive Charlotte and Jen, one heterosexual, one gay, both
from California, who found this small town inhospitable to the
single life. Then, arriving on the very first joint spousal appointment, there was brilliant Dee, whose son's birth coupled
with her husband's desertion hampered her research so she
did not receive tenure; lonely Eileen, the only African American in the department, plagued by family and health problems
until she took early retirement; and statuesque Carolyn, whose
distress over a tenure struggle did not diminish after it was
awarded and who now battles ovarian cancer. During those
lean times in the academy, when only one person would be

hired each year, together they seemed to stand for the decima-
tion of an entire generation, a legion of absences I dared not
disown. None remained; they had vanished, not as shockingly
as Chloe (I winced: "every six minutes," "44 percent"), but
with grave consequences nevertheless; and the rows of empty
parked cars seemed for the moment hearses, and the sparrows
fluttering a requiem for selves that had also been mine, those
who had suffered and thought intensely, and now a new time
was coming into being, made of the dust of generations following generations.

For the experiences of the "wives" and the "cohorts," fil-
tering down through layer upon layer of my reflections, saddened me, but curiously also strengthened my resolution to
support women's determination to pluck the tart bright fruits
of art and knowledge. It was not that I admired or befriended
them all, but my life was based upon theirs; I was one of the
many inheritors, one of the many continuers, one of the many
persons appointed to carry it on. And what luck that now there
were flocks of younger women from whom I could learn. So I
tried to bolster myself through instruction: time has passed,
my dear, but tomorrow the next generation must have a chance
for something better. Because of my own training in and love
of literature, I decided when I finally espied my car with its antique decal—a fish on a bicycle—I would remain in the English
department, but I would defy the shrinkage of age by support-
ing a gender studies department in all ways possible—maybe
with cross-listed courses, maybe with a joint appointment,
maybe by taking on some administrative duties. How can we
criticize or change higher education, if we do not become part
of its business-as-usual, I concluded. Gender studies would

need sponsors, if Myeong-Sook was right about her last stage;
perhaps the institutionalization of feminism would make it
seem as dated and dull as its detractors have always tried to
make it appear throughout its long evolution.

It was not a feminist but a cultural studies scholar friendly
to feminism, Stuart Hall, who described institutionalization as
a moment of profound danger and then added "dangers are not
places you run away from but places that you go towards." And
so I reflected as I unlocked my car, though I may be too old to
run toward danger, though I am wary of becoming an insider
in just about any club, though I seemed caught in a retrospec-
tive, self-reflexive loop (thinking less about sex and gender
and sexuality, more about how we have thought about sex and
gender and sexuality), the twenty-five years had passed in the
blink of an eye, but women need another twenty-five years and
then again another to test and measure themselves in the academy. There is no mark on the wall to gauge the precise height
of professional women, no yardstick, neatly divided into frac-
tions of an inch, that one can lay against the qualities of a good
dean, or the devotion of a librarian, or the fidelity of an editor,
or the capacity of an advisor. I resolved then, even if the gains
of women in higher education serve the good only of women in
higher education (which I emphatically did not and do not believe), they are worth the price of institutionalization, for the
rash revolt of optimism sometimes has to be justified against
the superior plausibilities of pessimism. With Bill's spoofing
in mind, I swung open the door, murmuring the sort of words
one hears at the end of a drug spot on the evening news, right
before the voice-over detailing its deleterious side effects (mi-
graines, flatulence, ulcers, neuropathies, bladder leakage!):
"it's our future, so we'd better be there."

CHAPTER 6

REPRODUCTION IN AN AGE OF
MECHANICAL PRODUCTION

ON ONE propitious day that next summer, the light of June was flooding the countryside, and the hum of traffic lessened as I turned off the highway with its hideous new condominium complexes onto Elvedon Road. Soon my decrepit car bumped down a deeply rutted driveway, where a clapboard bungalow stood, with old-fashioned long windows and a rickety front porch. It was only a matter of time, I thought conclusively as the most fertile season in the Midwest showed itself to be all one could want—teeming, amorous, creative. Encircling the house was a stubby lawn, but behind the house and beyond the lawn an orchard appeared, bordered by an infinity of smoke bushes crowded with tender new growth; asters and nasturtiums sprouted among the red-veined leaves of kale in an adjacent garden, where peas and beans, raspberries and marigolds, carrots and garlic were starting their maturation in neater beds. And beyond that one could just glimpse a long grassy meadow catching the gleams of golden afternoon light. The hot still day, the twentieth of June, was cooling down. I remember the date because exactly one month earlier I had found a fitting excuse once again not to join the endless processions at graduation, though I had attended the department's awards ceremony—I was delighted that both Nell and Arthur had won prizes. And the party seemed in part a celebration, of the freedom stretching before me, though of course its actual occasion was the baby's long-awaited appearance, but then why the costumes, and the elves?—or were they gnomes?

A table with assorted wines, beers, designer waters, and insect repellents had been set up on a wooden deck strewn with folding chairs, but only a handful of guests had arrived, most of them mingling on a lawn dotted with unlit candles held in high, baroque posts. Under two spreading tulip poplars, the string players were tuning up amid eccentric masquerades: several girls in brightly colored drapes, with brilliant paper flowers in their hair, had stepped straight out of a Gauguin canvas to chat with an Abyssinian prince, who seemed to be muttering something that sounded like "chuck-a-choi, chuck-a-choi"; in a flutter at being late, a mad March Hare put a paw out to a Greek goddess who might have been Clio or, for that matter, Sappho; mocking laughter issued from a Valkyrie conferring with Aspasia and a stately plump Queen Victoria whispering to Cleopatra, whose crown—inscribed "Queen of Denial"—was borne by a nun in full habit. When Marita, one of the Gauguin girls, saw me taking a heavy pot and a smaller bowl out of the back seat to balance them on the trunk, she hurried over to help. Because of her buzz cut, she wore her flowers as a sort of hat. I let her carry the fava beans Mona had given me so many months ago, but I would need mitts to hold the casserole, still hot from the oven, and probably I should have sampled both since I was fearful that, after months in the freezer, they might have lost their flavor or, worse still, might poison Mona's guests. Much to my sorrow, my aunt's year-long visitorship was coming to an end, along with her marriage. But that meant Melissa's stint in New York was also nearing completion, and, as I was instructed to put the food near the wine and beer, I found myself wondering if Melissa would be able to return in time to attend this celebration.

"I'm so glad to see you are wearing it," Marita exclaimed, openly eying the two-piece top she had brought back from New York as a gift for me. "The camisole works perfectly underneath, looks just great! Oh, but before I forget, Mona wanted you to have this." She handed over a sealed envelope.

The transparent sea green blouse felt strangely revealing to me so, after pocketing the envelope, I fidgeted with my Walter Benjamin glasses and hid my embarrassment beneath a shawl, but Marita snatched it away with a laugh, saying it spoiled the whole effect.

"I wasn't told to wear a costume," I groused to Marita, partly because of the self-consciousness I always feel at parties: my mother used to call me "the rubber band" when she would send me, then an adolescent, out into a crowded room only to discover I had snapped back immediately, to be plastered by her side; and this distress at social engagements escalated in later life, especially if I arrived too early, when just a few people talked loudly so as to try to convince themselves something pleasant would be sure to eventuate. Quite young, these guests seemed, and separate from me in their odd attire, absorbed with each other, or set on affairs that left me out entirely.

"This group is Mona's seminar," Marita explained, point-edly folding the shawl and stowing it with the mitts on a nearby chair. "We arrived early, in costume, to surprise her with some extra hands to do the setting up and serving." She must have sensed my discomfort and therefore pointed out the circu-itous paths around the orchard. I was being offered a respite, I realized with relief, and, noting a little seat almost hidden at the garden's edge, I leaped at the chance to mull over the complicated experiences of the day. Would it be impolite to absent myself in felicity for a while, I worried aloud, but, no, Marita was urging me to do just that while she and the others brought out the glasses, finished the chopping, arranged the salads, and Mona herself had gone to fetch the ice. So, pleased at being released, I took myself off, noting how the heat of the sun—winking on the berries and on vines with huge petals in various stages of gorging into zucchinis—would warm me after a very confusing meeting and thus put me into a more mirthful mood for the festivities to come. The stone itself had imbibed the sun's rays, I sensed, settling into my pastoral niche.

At this moment, as I sat half-hidden on the bench and as so often happens in the country, there was a complete lull and the sensation of being suspended in time. Nothing in the garden stirred; nobody came near. A single leaf detached it-self from the cascading plant beside me, and in that pause fell. Somehow it was like a signal pointing to a force in things that one had overlooked, a river that flowed invisibly through na-ture, and brought from the lawn or the driveway or the meadow two speckled butterflies (or were they moths?) circling higher and higher around the garden until one alighted, poised on the purple tip of a drooping spray of flowers on the branch at my eyes' level. Nor did the delicate visitor seem the least perturbed by my proximity, for it fastened to the tiny florets and displayed its astonishingly vivid coloring for some minutes before gliding off as if swept by the current elsewhere. Sitting in the hot sun, hearing now and again the buzz of a wasp, the hum of a bee hovering at the cup of a flower, and the small noises coming from the patio, my mind was fixed upon the strange opening and closing of the paper-thin wings, very slow they had seemed—I raised and lowered my index finger to capture that regular rhythm, overcome with awe that such a fragile yet boldly designed thing could exist at all. First it had danced overhead in the air, making its spotted colors flake, but once poised on its purple plush, it had pleated, then extended, pleated, then extended its patterned wings. In a world without professors or specialists, how peaceful it is rooted at the center, where there are no officious meddlers in lab coats measuring and weighing, sterilizing and injecting, screening and monitoring, fusing and flushing beside tangled heaps of vials, diagnostic printouts, catheters, chemical solutions, blinking and bleeping machines. I was overwhelmed that the garden seemed so deeply embedded in and with life, that the tongue-shaped leaves with the intense purple petals stirred in the summer breeze, and at my right foot—as if at another signal—a high-stepping angular insect, bright green, progressed toward the definite goal of crossing crumbs of loose earth, with its antennae trembling in deliberation, until it succeeded in creeping up out of the dirt, onto a browning leaf bent just low enough to form a bridge on which it could lodge.

Though the sights were ordinary enough, what was strange was the rhythmical sequence, the falling leaf, the papery flut-

terer at momentary stasis on the purplish stalk, and then at its
flight the chartreuse adventurer stepping stately off, a conti-
nuity that seemed to communicate something about the mysteries of the unity of nature. Perhaps to think, as I had been
thinking this past year, of gender as distinct from sex and of sex
as distinct from sexuality is an effort that interferes with the
unity of nature; but what exactly is nature, I wondered, recalling the curious project undertaken earlier that day by Morgan
(this was the name Dredlocks preferred over his given name).
What does one mean by a phrase like "the unity of nature," I
ruminated, for the egg donor programs and the artificial insemination clinics, the cyborgs and clones of the biomedical
technologies he wanted to study were so fantastic as to justify
his wanting me to help him understand a field of inquiry that
had to be directed by a biologist but might very well profit from
some readings in science fiction.

But, then, why meet in the newly constructed business
building, I had wondered while marveling at the lofty atrium
at the center of the building; the halls lined by set-in wooden
benches beside real potted plants; the seminar room rugged
in a nubby robin's blue with its capacious windows overlooking the arboretum; its high-tech DVD, video, and computer
gadgetry; its marble-topped square table surrounded by upholstered leather seats on casters, complete with armrests and
backs that could recline. In this sumptuous setting, redolent of
the Ivies (its door displayed the name of a beneficent patron),
Morgan had convened faculty I did not know—a biologist, a professor from the business school, another from the law school,
and myself—to map out a course of study in independent undergraduate research that proved to me how much I still had to

learn. For the talk about sheep, frog, and therapeutic cloning, commercial contract motherhood, Baby M, laparoscopy, the administration of ovulation, the cryopreservation of embryos, fetal reduction, nuclear transfers, stem cells, egg banks, postmortem ventilation therapies, SRY, and PGD sounded strange to my ears and, therefore, it was the lawyer who translated SRY into Sex-Determining Region Y gene, referring to the chromosome, and PGD into Pre-implantation Genetic Diagnosis, explaining that parents could now choose the sex of their babies; and it was the biologist who knew about coalitions between ecofeminists and FINRRAGE (Feminist International Network of Resistance to Reproductive and Genetic Engineering), an alliance of activists dedicated to the proposition that these technologies have worked and will inexorably continue to work so as to buttress male control over women's bodies.

I had done my homework and could therefore encourage Morgan to read those gender studies scholars grappling in multiple ways with biotechnology and the body. Indeed, I handed him a bibliography that listed titles by Ruth Bleier, Gena Corea, Sandra Harding, Valerie Hartouni, Katherine Hayles, Evelyn Fox Keller, Sadie Plant, Michelle Stanworth, Rosemarie Tong, Elizabeth Wilson, and many others. But my sense of their combined publications—hazy though it was—led me to feel that a number of these thinkers would not necessarily reject all diagnostic and screening procedures, and would certainly not spurn them on the basis of any sanctimonious return to "the unity of nature." Somewhat to my surprise, I had found that these theorists of "cyberfeminism" and "the posthuman," "reproductive technologies" and "cognitive neurology" gauged not only science's potential for helping women (with infertility, pregnancy, or aging-related problems) but also its capacity for making manifest precisely how unnatural nature is (and will continue to be in times to come). If misused, efforts to monitor or control menarche, menstruation, ovulation, pregnancy, lactation, and menopause might certainly undermine women's authority over their own bodies, could undoubtedly contribute to sinister forms of surveillance, probably would create physical problems related to those they sought to solve; however, the prospect of scientific advance usually holds out the promise of healing more than it hurts, and, in any case, could it be, had it ever been halted?

What might it mean, I heard a voice ringing in my inner ear as the angular green insect stepped up the brown leaf toward a thick juicy stalk, that we seem to be in the process of devising methods by which women may bear children without men, men might bear children without women? Some infants can now be born without a father: consider the baby conceived by means of artificial insemination in the womb of a married woman whose husband assumes legal paternity, though he has absolutely no genetic link to the child. Despite the intermittent interference of judges set upon establishing a donor's juridical rights, artificial insemination can and does play havoc with patrilineal descent, allowing single women to establish families of their own, families without men. Some infants can now be born with two "natural" mothers: consider the baby beginning within one woman's egg—either *in vivo* (within the body) or *in vitro* (in glass)—then transferred and implanted into another woman's womb. Both the egg-producing (genetic) mother and the pregnant (gestational) mother could be said to be embroiled in some (if not all) stages of biological maternity. If infants can be birthed or adopted and reared by two loving mothers or two loving fathers, lineage as we know it will alter, will bring entirely new kinship patterns (and perhaps different psychologies and perspectives) into being. Although this was not one of Morgan's concerns, I had read that in the Netherlands, as in France, Denmark, Massachusetts, and Canada, same-sex couples have received all or some of the rights attached to marriage. But elsewhere, I knew, too many adults feel split off or held back from relationships that would fulfill their lives, unable to secure the new family relationships they were in the process of fashioning. Yet these instances, especially in Holland, prove the possibility of rearranged social orders in which all can continue without effort because nothing need be hidden, twisted, or repressed. And this perhaps, I surmised, glancing again at the purple-plumed bush, is illustrative. Was the bush with its drooping clusters hermaphroditic, like the vast majority of flowering plants, and was its gender—biologists spoke of phenotypic gender or functional gender—determined by the proportion of its flowers with egg or sperm cells? Didn't the gender of plants depend on the environment, on the seasons, on pollination, on neighboring plants? Certainly when I saw the insect alight and attach itself in a natural fusion with the florets, "the unity of nature" spoke about odd couplings of marvelously dissimilar, even unlikely forms of life. The delicate high flyer—did it alight to feed, to rest, to warm up, to mate?—might have laid its egg (or is it eggs?) on the plant. In which case, a legless grub would eventually emerge to eat part of the bush so as to build its cocoon and begin its mystic transmutation. The mutuality of the plant consumed to become a sort of womb, the bush or tree protecting larvae until pupae emerge, the butterfly or moth or wasp hatched with its sticky tremulous wings, its survival assured even in the absence of its mother: what does it signify?

One has a profound, if irrational, instinct in favor of the theory that all sorts of permutations make for great satisfactions, complicated joys. A droning near my ear, the angular chartreuse insect just at this moment blending invisibly on the thick stalk, the bee humming at the yellow petals, and the pleasure of the sun's rays gave me pause. Recalling the research into human sexuality begun so many decades ago at my own school, I wondered, didn't most insects and many animals survive because of caretaking undertaken by those not directly involved in birthing? "Allomothers" was the term Sarah Blaffer Hrdy used, "meaning all the caretakers other than the mother . . . who help care for or provision young." Could flimsy gall moths survive at all without goldenrod or a huge and tough oak tree serving as allomother? Why had "agamic" generations of the gall, which can reproduce without sexual union, been placed in a totally separate genus, as if they weren't galls at all? And did mighty oak trees have a gender or a sex, I wondered, and if so, what would that mean to the gall?

When people create caretaking households (for the young, for the old) so varied as to reshape the very idea of the family, when new words will have to be invented to describe the roles nurturers play, will the desire circulating in such unions be regulated by conventional ideas about gender or sex or sexuality? Should such women and men gain equal rights to marriage, child custody, adoption, foster care, and fertility services, nuclear families will be quickened by the proliferation of arrangements governing ever more diverse forms of parenting, no longer defined in terms of mothering and fathering. What differences might eventuate in terms of the gender affiliations or the sexual orientations or the psychological well-being of all these children—if any? Whether or not they contribute to the health and happiness of future generations, proliferating technologies will alter our conceptualizations of human intercourse along with our definitions of kinship, though I had to admit that the science fiction I brought to Morgan's attention did not bode well in this regard.

"Hello, what happened to you?" I asked in some surprise at the sadly shorn and thus diminished replica of Pinka who thrust his nozzle into my lap, just as once again I thought I caught a glimpse of two diminutive beings—sprites? fairies?— in colorful caps. Why had the golden coat been sacrificed—he had been clipped all over into a miniaturized semblance of himself—and was that why he seemed somewhat ashamed? He was nothing, nobody, his abject bald ears, shaved head, and attenuated legs seemed to say about his own disfigurement, as he first methodically licked each one of my fingers and then lay down in the grass to let the sun burn through his almost naked skin, roasting on one side, then another while I returned to my musings about science fiction; for, from *Frankenstein* to *The Handmaid's Tale* and *Bloodchild*, women's imaginative writings have emphasized the hideous progeny and monstrous violence men manufacture when they attempt to usurp the womb with a manmade incubator, the indignity suffered by people reduced to an underclass of exploited breeders of life they produce but do not possess.

New prenatal technologies—egg retrieval and embryo implantation, amniocentesis and sonography, fetal monitoring and genetic diagnosis—might subject women to humiliating dependency on medical experts (still mostly male) more concerned with the production of the perfect fetus ("perfect," by whose standards?) than the reproduction of the woman (and wouldn't she and her infant suffer far graver risks if she were black and poor or from the third world?). As if she were privy to the skepticism of the fiction writers, the lawyer at Morgan's meeting—citing the work on intersectionality by Kimberlé Crenshaw, Patricia Hill Collins, and Patricia J. Williams—had reviewed a host of rulings about bizarre conflict-of-interest cases between a surrogate mother and the zygote's legal parents, over the ownership of frozen fertilized eggs after the death of the sperm- or egg-donor, about the relative "market value" (a grotesque phrase) of black versus white eggs, sperm, and infants.

Stroking Pinka's forlorn head and heeding the distant clinking of glasses, I recalled making my way out of Morgan's meeting through corridors in which nobody was reading *Frankenstein;* it seemed that the School of Business was wholly indifferent to Mary Shelley's assumption that the offspring propagated by a mad doctor would suffer from loneliness and anguish over its own constructedness. Nobody cared a straw— and I tried not to blame them—for the past or future of feminist responses to medical technology. But, I suspected, if the stock advances or declines of pharmaceutical companies, egg- and sperm-banks, and fertility and sex selection clinics, as well as the instrument and chemical industries and hospital firms that served them, had been chalked on the pavement, hurrying feet would have stopped to consider whether the economy was going toward a downward spiral or quickening into an upturn. If the drug companies and the body-parts salesmen and the managers of health insurance in the myriad companies seeking to prolong life, if the multi-billion-dollar corporations dealing with assisted care and old-age institutions prospered, the numbers would be digitally displayed from the rooftops, a cause of celebration, regardless of the ethical issues they raised. In 1980, Australia's first test-tube baby cost $1,500,000, which was why, I realized, the business faculty member had been enlisted, why I was privileged to witness the schism not, as in the old days, between the humanities and the sciences but between the impoverishment of the college of arts and sciences, on the one hand, and the wealth of the professional schools, on the other.

But if the faculty in the business building cared only about the commercial consequences of biotechnology, wasn't it possible that many of the most conservative voices so prominent in society today—"family values" and "pro-life" advocates, legislators trying to pass measures that would require schoolteachers to label homosexuality "perverse," televangelists preaching the ordained submission of women to men, lobbyists for a marriage amendment to the Constitution and abstinence-only sex education, war hawks, creationists opposed to the teaching of evolution—may have come into prominence as a reflex against growing uncertainty about what constitutes human life, from where or exactly when its origins spring, as might the tenacity with which so many hold on to religious maxims split off from any faith informing their everyday lives.

No age can ever have been as stridently dedicated to policing, displaying, analyzing, promoting, publicizing sex-consciousness as our own; those innumerable books by and about

men on Amazon.com are a proof of it, as are the proliferation
of pornographic images on the Internet and on the higher
channels of cable TV. Biological investigations and experi-
ments were no doubt in part to blame. They must have roused
in men and women an extraordinary anxiety about what constitutes the human; must have made them lay an emphasis
upon men needing women, women needing men, on the marriage of opposites being consummated or the romance of the
sexes cooperating, on the complementarity of masculinity and
femininity, on the healthy fusion of sexual reproduction, gender duality, and heterosexual desire that they would not have
troubled to think about had they not been challenged by biologists and those journalists who make their findings available
to the larger public, and also by feminists and queer theorists.
For when one is challenged, even if by a few scientists, science
writers, and academic kooks, one retaliates, sometimes rather
excessively.

That Pinka waved his tail, if sheepishly, at this moment
may explain my own intuition that Evie was approaching, but
why did he cower away, as if from a disgusting sight, and at a
presence that usually brought him such joy? She came running
full tilt toward me, though somewhat unbalanced by the bun-
dle in her arms. All aglow with happiness was Evie, laughing
but quietly since the infant in its swaddling blanket was fast
asleep, for she wanted me to come with her back to the patio, to
Harry, who (it seemed) had some plan afoot that had to be accomplished while the brilliant sky remained blue, though pink
now tinged the edges of puffs of clouds scattered on the hori-
zon. As we made our way back to the more densely populated
patio, Evie was rueful, recounting Pinka's reaction to the new

arrival in their apartment, how he refused to be tempted by the usual treats or attentions, how instead he recoiled as if from a repulsive presence, then sniffed and strutted about to contrast his own independence with the helpless, puling, bleating lump in Evie's arms. The summer haircut had been the final straw, she explained, plummeting Pinka into a deep depression.

Mona, in a royal-blue and silver sari, handed me a glass of wine, while Evie tried to move the baby from one arm to the other without waking her. But Harry intervened, lifting the sleepy infant and holding her up, brandishing her like a precious chalice before the masqueraders and the gathering guests, for all the world as if to say, "Well, though she looks asleep to us, she has flown across the globe to reach us and has seen what the earth looks like, and now she is choosing her kingdom, for she has agreed that she will rule over that territory without coveting any other and will grow up with few illusions about other people and absolutely none about herself." In the words he actually uttered, though, he proposed a toast to congratulate Evie and welcome her baby: "To womanhood," he called out to those within earshot, "in its infancy, in its young adulthood; may women grow into their maturity." After I peeked at the little extraterrestrial—tightly wound up in light cotton; its delicate fingers curled like tendrils; its velvet skin unmarked; its blank, bright eyes staring with the marbled innocence of sculpture—I lifted my glass and reflected on Harry's commitment to the baby, which was not merely ceremonial, for he had drawn up and signed papers attesting to his responsibilities and rights not exactly as a co-parent, more as a dependable brother or uncle. But I was realizing, too, that I could hardly imagine all the private scenes, the quarrels, the

moments of happiness, the changes as she grew that would give
Evie what I had never had, never would have.

"Hello?!" An aged man waiting to be given a drink called
out to me. "Don't you know me, even close up?" As a girl young
enough to be his granddaughter brought him a bottle of beer,
he smiled and added, "I had the distinct impression you did
not recognize us last spring . . . do you remember, we waved
and waved at you—stirred our stumps? What's the line about
the retired who neither die nor fade away? 'Forgotten, but not
gone!'"

He turned, chuckling toward a new arrival, as I thought
about the odd androgyny of the elderly. So it had been Professor Stevens and his granddaughter I had glimpsed getting into
a cab the afternoon I had observed Marita teaching, I realized
as new arrivals in search of drinks propelled me to the patio's
edge, where a ribboned rattan bassinet had been moved and
Harry was helping put a sling on Evie, who clearly could not
bear to put the baby down. The passage of years—the ancient
scholar needed a cane now, preserving hardly a trace of the
intrepid explorer—and Evie ambling away in proud harness
made me feel my own singularity, for there I was on the edge
of the party, like Addie inspecting the bulletin boards, noting
that the faculty were not mingling with the students, that no
one went to help take rickety Professor Stevens off his granddaughter's hands. Sinking his voice, Harry murmured the latest account of the police investigations into Chloe's fate: they
now believed Chloe had been accidentally hit by a van driven
by a couple who disposed of her body; divers had begun work
in the lake with what was described as "side-scan sonar equipment." It was intolerable, her body thrown away to coil and

curl aimlessly in the mud: no casket, no burial, no gravestone, no inscription. What the complete or matured person would have been, might have done, one can only surmise.

The party would be a failure—the full import of Chloe's death, I realized then and know again now, can never be comprehended—a complete fiasco: Melissa would never arrive in time, Mona was leaving for good, and, as for the baby, there would be Marta Wheaton coming in her mourning garb to denounce transnational adoption as a flagrant instance of American cultural imperialism similar to, for instance, Chinese women in bathing suits at the Miss World contest or a compound in the Afghan Ministry of Women's Affairs teaching makeup, manicures, pedicures, waxing, and hair styling. Why, then, did she come, merely to criticize? Or, I could not but reconsider, bearing in mind the inanity of beauty pageants and Marta's refusal to be checked by rejection or chilled by difficulty, had I resented her because she did risk her own point of view with zeal not misplaced, because she made me judge Evie and myself guilty, driving home the thought always nagging at the edges of my own mind, that one could not have such a gathering in many other spots on the globe and perhaps one should not on this green and pleasant bit of earth since the powers that be had decreed that wars would be waged, but waged elsewhere, far away, with casualties in foreign lands, with darker skins and strange-sounding names?

For isn't it this thought that wakes me in the middle of the night, making me leap up in anguish—the easy but habitual crime of omission, of failing to find a way to imagine doing something constructive, of knowing the world desperate but still rambling down back roads? I might like to think that my teaching effects some sort of political intervention, but vast amounts of monies are being spent not on the forty million Americans without healthcare coverage but on unfeasible missile defense systems. I might bristle at Marta Wheaton's strident diatribes against "neo-liberal consumerist feminism," yet didn't too many people—in my school, but elsewhere too—believe that being a feminist means being able to buy whatever you want? And wasn't it the case that too many people—in my school, but elsewhere too—fear that behind all the talk of Global Democracy—the capital letters themselves a cause of embarrassment—our own beloved country has been guilty of launching an age to come of pure, of self-assertive consumerism and arrogance? It was a shock (to those of us with faith in education) to see the faces of our elected leaders so stupid. Yes, I knew, Marta has important work to do when people like me and Evie want to be sheltered amid the tyranny, brutality, torture, and the worst threat, the end of freedom. Or, to be fairer, when people like me and Evie are too taken up with pressing private concerns: my mother would need more help eating, dressing, bathing, and if I could not pay for it, I would have to provide it myself.

No one but me, I suspected, would recognize "The March of the Women" being performed by the string players. For what did the prominence of "family values" and "pro-life" advocates, homophobic legislators, televangelists, war hawks, and creationists signify if not the grotesque paradox that feminists had entered higher education not only when Western culture discounted its value, but also when women's grass-roots movements outside the academy had been pronounced dead and buried on the covers of countless news magazines, in the evening talk shows of innumerable television stations? Were we in danger of losing even the few safeguards we had managed to get legislators and judges to authorize? As bolts of orange streaked the sky, it made me feel quite sick to know that the party was falling flat. Those people not seated on plastic or folding chairs wandered aimlessly off the patio onto the lawn, standing like stakes in scattered formations, not sure they would stay for dinner, silently thinking that perhaps they could find an excuse to leave early. Izzy and his wife, looking pained or perhaps only bored with glasses in hand, must have felt that something was lacking. I avoided exchanges with this shy student or that aggrieved colleague, feeling oppressed by a sense of being past everything, through everything, out of it. Mona and her son, listening to Bill talk about the influence of someone on anybody, knew that something was lacking, but what was it, they must have asked themselves. While damp cubes of cheese fell into mouths opening like post boxes, nothing and no one seemed to merge.

Melancholy were the scraps of talk hanging soiled in the air before each lonely skeleton of habit. "Because she interpretates way too much, like, most kids cut . . . number-one basketball and party school . . . it was so not wheat here, just brush and forest . . . offering Milly Brush peanuts over there? . . . she, not Marta, will chair gender studies . . . fifty thousand Darfurians killed . . . she writes for them, so they don't dare contest her . . . a female officer torturing an Iraqi prisoner? . . . one-sixth of the world population in slums . . . through my earbuds—'Earn a Degree without Interrupting Your Life!'. . . a bombing *where?* . . ."

All stood or sat separate, and the whole effort of creating a

sense of community seemed as impossibly futile as Morgan's
efforts to stop the clock. How misguided had been my original
impression of him, I recalled. He had determined to embark
on his independent course of study after reading Baudrillard;
what was the sentence? That "first sex was liberated from reproduction; today it is reproduction that is liberated from
sex"? What troubled Morgan, I knew from previous conversations with him, was the idea that biotechnological engineering
drained sexuality of its centrality in human existence. To Morgan, the coming of the human clone heralded the commodifi-
cation of an offspring constructed as a twin of its narcissistic
parent or manufactured as a perfected piece of portable state
property; the splicing of a rabbit with a jellyfish filled him with
horror—it had been done, he assured me; he had seen photos
in a museum installation. As I considered whether to move a
pan or sheet of (what could that be?) spareribs on a side table
crowded with cookies and éclairs and Bartlett pears, I agreed
with him about cloning, for there was something ghastly about
self-replication, the sameness of genetically simulated Xeroxed copies bred in accordance with some grotesque eugenic
ideal that would surely end up being just as lethal as it had been
in the "ethnic cleansing" two of Morgan's grandparents had not
managed to escape. But, I thought, he had probably only seen
some Photoshop rabbit-jellyfish collage; and in any case, giv-
en my understanding of Evie's fierce desire for a child—of the
difference she would undoubtedly make in the life of this particular baby girl—it would be absurd to equate single or same-
sex parenting with cloning or, for that matter, with transgenic
organisms.

Empty glass in hand, I left and moved on—on closer inspection it appeared that the baking sheet with ribs was a cleverly decorated chocolate cake—past a small cluster of adjuncts and teaching assistants. "Called Neve Shalom/Wahat al-Salam, or Oasis of Peace . . . *Amádan*, why don't we have paid family leaves, the way they do? . . . the tenure vs. the biological clock . . . older men's power a turn-on, but women's? . . . as a woman, I have a country I love, a government I fear . . . two-thirds of women with AIDS in this country are black . . . did you hear that orange is the next black? . . . that upping to orange came from disinformation . . . just the thought of nuclear terrorists . . . so I joined Code Pink, and Axis of Eve . . . known as *parité* . . . check made out to the Global Fund for Women . . . but *we* are the ones forty-third in infant mortality . . ." Words fluttered and swirled, while I moved toward a circle of quite young freshmen and sophomores and the table laden with main courses, for, wreathed about with chatter, I was brooding on the lengthening shadows, feeling the emptiness and the strain. Was there no safety, no learning to rely upon, no guide, I worried, tasting the fava beans to test their flavor, to see if they had spoiled or turned to paste.

Could it be, even for those as old as I have become, that this life—startling, unexpected—only looked more and more perplexing to people of good will who have to contend with profound differences of opinions adhering to our changing sense of ourselves and our world? Though it was not what had motivated Morgan, his project gave me a new slant on the abiding concerns of feminism. Neither biological determinism (the "essential" body in isolation) nor cultural determinism (the "socially constructed" subject), neither race alone nor nation, but neurological, biochemical, or genetic interactions with

psychological, social, political, and economic factors constitute men's and women's ways of being and knowing: heart,
body, brain, and world all mixed together and not contained
in separate compartments—this may be where investigators
would be going; and spirit too—our inattention had allowed religion to be hijacked by the right, where it intoned its age-old
refrains of "you shan't do this, you ought not do that," instead
of chanting its age-old hymns of peace and justice on earth,
freedom from want and despair.

With the light fading this quickly, I realized, I had better take advantage of it to read Mona's note so I tore open the
envelope, which contained a brief message to the effect that
a job in Chicana studies had opened up in the last minute;
Mona herself had written for Marita, but my letter could be
more specific about her teaching skills; and where it was to be
sent; timing was crucial—it would have to be mailed asap—and
we should keep our fingers crossed. The undergraduates near
me (yes, there were Nell and Olivia), did their nods mean they
could sense my pleasure at Marita's prospects, at Mona's exertions? "Where's that adorable baby from? . . . not Britney
Spears, Missy Elliott . . . they will drain that part of the lake if
they have to . . . *nu pretinde ca ceea ce nu ai nu are valoare* . . .
now they are saying a woman should stay home and breastfeed
or else the kid will be damaged and the mother will get breast
cancer . . . amandabright@home . . . cyber-sex in hyper-text?
. . . I'm freaked I'm not supposed to enjoy babies or baking . . .
like I'm still grossed I ought to . . . guilt, the gift that keeps on
giving . . . isn't he a metrosexual! . . . with Perfectmatch.com
. . . depends what you mean by beauty . . . and *The L Word?* . . .
it's the F word, sheroes . . . yeah, girl-on-girl assaults . . ."

As the sky darkened, a breeze swept around a small cluster of returning (older) students closer to the string players, who had begun a medley of spirituals, with the cello taking the part of Jessye Norman ("Now do you call that a sister?") and the violins playing Kathleen Battle's part ("No, No!") and the viola adding the refrain: "She scandalized my name." It was time to decide to rush off with an excuse or stay to celebrate, the guests must have been speculating, for they turned their wrists cautiously so they could read their watches. I suspected that many of them felt exactly as I did, plagued by an unreal sense of needing to be someone else. "But it is hard to remember what used to have to be," the old cronies chatted: "When the boy had to phone first . . . there were no female rabbis . . . when you couldn't go to a movie by yourself . . . then she was in sales, a traveler knocking on doors; now she's vice-president . . . fleas or sibling rivalry? . . . abortions botched, illegal in a deserted dentist's office at 10 P.M., for cash in hand . . . but twelve marines blown up, three of them women . . . the course at Smith was called 'Gracious Living' (was it required?)—how to set the table, what sorts of linens to use . . . only way to get tenure was a sex discrimination lawsuit . . . you were Mrs. or Miss . . . guys still can't wear skirts . . . *cante ista*, in the Lakota language . . . it's too early to tell . . ."

The stray voices I was half-hearing rustled with the trees and the bushes, sounding symbolic to my ears, as the tune changed to jazz and the rhythm kicked up to a campy rendition of "I Want a Girl Just Like the Girl Who Married Dear Old Dad." "We think back through our friends and their families . . . through journalists ('wildings' never happened) . . . salsa, anyone? . . . we couldn't think back without Virago and Naiad

. . . what about thinking forward, Resolution 1325? . . . they call him 'bio-pop'. . . not your parents, it's your birth order . . . do you remember *Chrysalis?* . . . equivalent word for 'uxorious' . . . *che lavoro fa?* . . . Googling Combahee River Collective . . . with *Las Madres del Plaza de Mayo* . . . met at a donor sibling registry . . . shades of Shulamith . . ." When Sappho, Queen Victoria, and the Abyssinian prince went about lighting the candles held aloft in their posts and stuck into the lawn, the whole scene might have floated off in carnival.

Was it the second glass of wine or the luminous halo of the candles or had the talk started to reverberate with the strings because of another crescendo, actually two: first the odd honkings of (could it be?) a flock of geese (passing overhead or in a neighboring hollow?), which was followed by that curious twittering birds sometimes seem to call forth from each other as they herald the end of light, the coming of the dusky blue deepening into darkness. It was the time when colors undergo their intensification; when the beauty of the world revealed and yet so soon to perish has the effect of making one feel there is no need to hurry, to sparkle, to be someone else. Whether because of the treble syllabling from the birds' goodnight or the discordant honkings of the neighboring geese or that particularly bluish-black sky that always entrances, they kept on talking so it would not be a failure, after all; it would be all right and it had begun, there was no doubting that, I thought, watching more students and faculty arrive, many with children in tow—young and old assembling, some with expressions of surprise, as if to say, "I'm here, though my grandmother wouldn't have been invited, my great-grandfather either."

The upright flames of the candles glowing around the patio drew the guests together, even those on the lawn, brought the faces nearer, so many became aware of making a party together on this common ground in the twilight, as the sky purpled overhead. And now I thought, trying to analyze the cause of the sudden exhilaration, Melissa will arrive, for anything might happen, I sensed, imagining some future time when the baby would be set on Pinka's back and Pinka would trot about with the baby pulling his tail, and he would submit with grace, and would discover that the baby's affections were returned in full, for (he would suspect) did not the baby somehow resemble Pinka, Pinka the baby? Hearing the volume of babble rise around me, I considered the women's movement outside the academy, pronounced dead and buried by talking heads; but, I understood, these women and men here, like those outside institutions of higher education, are embarked on decidedly experimental lives. Yes, we would have to protect the safeguards we had managed to get legislators and judges to authorize, and continue organizing for other rights and laws as well; but perhaps now, as before, feminism—a predominantly political movement against the oppression of many differently situated women—ramifies also through the personal and professional decisions made by scores of variously stationed people, all bringing into being more egalitarian arrangements, though this vague formulation hardly seemed to sum it up.

I drifted among small groups of people, remembering Marita's class on "Fantomina," Mona's influence on the conference panelists, what I had gleaned from my arguments with Melissa and Marta Wheaton, as I eavesdropped on a gigantic conversation. "On LambdaMOO! . . . 'a uterus is not a substitute for a conscience'. . . is it any better if a female professor hits on an undergraduate? . . . he would give her an A, if she pulled down her panties and . . . in Ehrenreich, or was it Pollitt? . . . yes, everyone is always quoting her, with the result that I resolved never to read a line . . . Vita, Boink, H Bomb . . . no cookies till after dinner . . . the book has to be adapted to the technology . . . the priests' pederasty or the bishops' cover-ups? . . . stuck at *The Second Shift* . . . more than one of us is missing . . . she's called a doula . . ."

What it amounts to is that feminism has gained in self-consciousness—feminists, that is to say, are able to disagree with each other so vigorously that, for all the quibbling and quarreling, there was never a dull moment during the past year. For when one takes feminism's ideas into the mind, they swell with significance, they gush and pour, giving forth all kinds of other ideas, and that is the sort of thinking and writing of which one can say that it has the secret of perpetual life. "When the Daughters of Bilitis expelled Beth Elliott . . . virus in the spam? . . . they're called 'post-feminists'. . . the black equivalents of Bella Abzug, Gloria Steinem, Betty Friedan? . . . protesting the 'Lavender Menace' at NOW . . . forty million Americans are functionally illiterate . . . anything edible for a vegan? . . . the courage of an Ayaan Hirsi Ali . . . 'Not Ready to Make Nice' . . . the spirit of the Girlie-girl, the Guerrilla Girls . . . *chicanisma!* . . ."

But whatever the reason may be, I realized as I put down my wine glass to accept another, smaller glass, it is a fact today that not all of the books by men celebrate only male virtues, enforce only male values, or describe only the world of men; indeed, we no longer know what "male virtues" or "male values" or "the world of men" might be, despite the pronouncements of old codgers who enliven conversation by mourning the death of what they call real men, real women; despite the advertisements of Marlboro and Victoria's Secret. Nonsense, I thought, the new arts of living women and living men are only just coming into existence, the children and foster children and godchildren, the graduate students and undergraduates of feminists: women who need no longer lay great stress on their grievances in the most boringly predictable manner, men who no longer need to assert their superiority in the most boringly predictable manner. "A *jeu*, a love letter, a romp . . . but how she hated 'their nasal voices, and their oriental jewelry, and their noses, and their wattles'. . . why must one always write like somebody else? . . just American feel-goodism . . . so much changed, and yet so little . . . there *was* a female Crick and Watson . . . re-articulation, not unanimity . . . fascist prowar poems, reams by women . . . I'd take Iris Murdoch over Rawls any day . . . harder questions neither asked nor answered . . . let's keep on going . . ."

While I rambled—my reflections punctuated by the overheard chatter, feeling dizzy from the buzzing in my ears and tipsy from the wine, peering at the oddly colored liquid in the small glass that had been placed in my hand, no longer doubtful about the need to eat something and soon—I heard Melissa's voice calling me and then there she was, after all those months, still lustrous, and we kissed first this cheek, then that, and then the first again (because Melissa, I remembered, believed this third extra kiss brought good luck), while Marta Wheaton appeared to herd us toward the food table where Evie now wanted to make a toast of her own. Despite the lively toddler tugging at Marta's tresses and wiggling to escape her hold, she was leading a raggle-taggle group of children—they were the ones I had taken to be elves—who were quickly directed to position themselves in a semicircle before her. As the rest of us looked on, one soft tone from a pitch pipe, and then words without associations, hauntingly enigmatic sounds—"Tee-na sez way, Tee-na sez way"—filled our ears with the tremulous sweetness produced only by youthful voices singing out of doors in an a cappella chorus. With the last harmonies quavering in the serene air, Marta promised one more folksong now and more later in the evening from this troupe, which had formed out of those boys and girls who had benefited from Chloe's volunteer work at the hospital and who, Marta explained, were therefore performing concerts to raise money to fund a scholarship in her name (for an undergraduate concentrating in the medical humanities).

The child Marta handed to a companion (her partner?) was a surprise, the scholarship and singers too; and now, as I found myself listening to another African melody, I wondered if perhaps Marta's single-mindedness might have been the result of her simply having to be as efficient with her time as possible; and why not simply be efficient—with no emoting, smoothing of ruffled feathers, proffering of tea and sympathy, I asked myself, as Marta's ability to think outside herself and outside patterns oppressive to others struck me as the source of her activism. Though I tingled with the revelation of the good office she had undertaken for Chloe and for the anonymous singers—the brave recipients of Chloe's care—and also with all those feelings that swell the nerves and thrill the spine and affect the sight, the very visceral pleasures of the reunion of friends, I expressed my gladness only by asking Melissa in a whisper if she was also starved. Joined by Mona and Marita, I stood beside Melissa, vibrating with the fluttering, alive sound of Marta's choir but also feeling that I was more firmly attached to all of them than colleagues ordinarily are—not in a personal sense, but in a more capacious, more porous and disinterested way; and wondering, do we have the same pairs of eyes, only different spectacles, for I never stop thinking of them, what they might perceive differently through their lenses and how that might color the picture, or sharpen the focus, or change the frame of my own views.

One wanted their eyes and fifty more pairs of eyes to see with, I reflected, for each pair of eyes peering simultaneously makes its own contributions, and even all those were insufficient to get around the complexity of the issues we face and will continue to face. Looking at them and beyond them to the others milling about, I came to feel how difficult it is to collect oneself into one person, for they were all in some sense parts of me, or rather, of the sense of contiguity among us. They widened my landscape amid the flickering candles and now a lone star quivering in the night sky. Did it matter that it must end for my mother, that I too would inevitably cease completely? All this will go on without us; was it not consoling that each survives, spun out in fine filaments like mist between people hardly known? Even Chloe, I thought watching the haze over the feathery spears mounding at the end of the meadow, lives in the tremulous vibratos filling the air, in the memories of the children whose songs will merge suspended in the tall grasses, the sloping hillside, the lilacs that droop in May, the ferns that lift their delicate tendrils by the banks of the lake, when the frogs croak along with the crickets in the August night, and in the bright hush, the blank solemnity of all these here now, for she and those assembled are somehow successive and continuous. What they and my sense of intellectual intimacy with them give to me is an illusion of the unseen parts of myself surviving, attached to this or that person, and the new being we were welcoming—making the world dance. The significance of that rhythm, heaven knows I can't guess, but there is significance—that I feel overwhelmingly. Perhaps with my limitations, all I can do is gesture toward what I understood then and today still feel to have been the romance, yes the love affair of my life.

When Marta bowed first to Melissa, then to me, I realized that she liked us better than she ever had before and wondered—with a feeling of relief and gratitude—at this chivalry we had begun to exhibit with each other, so I bowed back as best I could, pleased at how seriously we took our attentiveness to one another. Though Evie clearly wanted to address those finally assembled, Melissa—who had a book in her hand—turned the pages until she found the passage she needed and, with the air of one who was pleased to be doing what she had earlier determined to do and the graceful poise I always so admired in her, recited in an Italian Mona then translated:

> per quanti si dice più lì "nostro,"
> tanto possiede più di ben ciascuno.

> for by so many more there are who say "our"
> So much the more of good doth each possess.

The liquor tasted sweet on my lips (was it some sort of apricot cocktail?), as an affable hawk could barely be seen circling over the head of a distant student who might have been Myeong-Sook or Arthur. But Evie, having handed the baby over to Harry, was finally speaking with her usual energy and candor.

"First I want to thank you all for helping to make this celebration possible. Then I want to wish a fond farewell to Mona, a fond welcome to Melissa," she hugged each of them, "though you've both been with us in spirit this last year, and you both will continue to be in spirit with us this coming year." She raised her glass and sipped. "Harry wanted to name the baby 'Sophia,'" she continued, "a lovely name, but I always had it in my heart to call her after a beloved cousin, my second cousin Mary, and also a dear friend" (here she looked intently at me). "Mary Sophia she will be, and I don't know whether to laugh or cry with excitement; let's eat and drink and be merry together so as to continue working out our plans for the good of a world that none of us will ever know, but one we all hope Mary Sophia may enter."

There, I felt in a flush of pleasure and surprise, this is the wish we share, this striving forward, to add to the treasury of moments that will join congregations of past time, and, curiously too, this wanting to enclose the present moment, and make it persist; to fill it fuller and fuller (I put down the glass and looked for a ladle I had placed next to the brown pot) so the past would press against the present, the present against the future, until all shone with understanding. We are only just measuring in a long passage, I thought, moving a salt shaker closer to the *foul madamas* (probably everything had to be taken with a few grains of salt); and this pulsing partakes, I knew, carefully helping Melissa and myself to especially tender pieces of the *boeuf en daube*, of eternity; there is a permanence, a durability to our progress, a coherence that changes and yet stays the same in the face of the ephemeral and the spectral so that once again I had a feeling of the collaborations that endure in what feminists have brought about. While a multitude of bright tiny lights seemed to ascend and sparkle over the distant meadow, gliding like minute spots of desire, from all sides myriad impressions engaged my mind, composing in their sum what we might venture to call feminism itself, flooding me with a view of its infinite possibilities. When Marta's toddler and many of the other children then ran off, wanting to catch the fireflies in their hands, and the first notes (heralding the second, then the third) of the "Cavatina" rose from the string quartet seated beneath the lofty poplars, I experienced that breath of tenderness so very uncommon at a party, the sense of exquisite cordiality that makes one want to refrain from hurrying on but instead keep still to sum up and say to the moment, this very moment, stay, you are so fair.

Here, then, Mary Beton's story must cease. She has told you how she reached the conclusion that feminists have transformed higher education and how higher education has definitively transfigured the situations and conversations of women. She has left the great problems of the true nature of woman and the true goals of higher education unsolved, but she has asked you to follow her impressions while she was teaching and being taught by students and colleagues inside and outside her department. Flying in the face of media caricatures of academics, she has intimated that the distinctive groups formed within feminism can learn to live with their differences, as well as their differences of opinion, by forging alliances and coalitions based upon the political goals they share. As she was laying bare her thoughts, you have probably been observing her foibles and failures so as to decide how they influenced or circumscribed her opinions. Perhaps you have contested her ideas or extended them in some way she could not possibly have foreseen. At least this is what I hope, for I meant her story to demonstrate how truth can be understood only by laying together the errors, apprehensions, and conjectures of what Marta would call "embodied subjectivities" from various "positionalities" within the sometimes comic, sometimes tragic circumstances that shape human relationships under sundry atmospheres. Now, therefore, I will end if not exactly in my own voice then certainly not in Mary Beton's in order to anticipate two objections that cannot fail to arise.

Serious intellectual debates, you may say, cannot simply be reduced to a narrative about stock types in settings all too obviously inflected by one woman writer's oeuvre, no matter how wonderful a writer she may have been. Along these same lines, you might object that no seriously new advance in knowledge can be made without the footnotes and judicious specificity necessary for proper academic investigations, without all the careful reasoning and historical archiving one finds in articles published in flagship journals, a point to which I would readily and respectfully consent. But proper academic investigations with scrupulous reasoning and historical archiving abound; and while there may be no genuinely new directions for feminist inquiry proposed in these pages, it is just as important at this moment to grasp hold of the larger picture so as to map the contours of its shapes in a manner that rises above the fray of pitting this approach against that one, this methodology over another, the claiming of superiority or imputing of inferiority to various specialized fields and definitions of feminism.

Of course criticism has taken many a narrative turn before, though it was obviously Virginia Woolf's *A Room of One's*

Own and (to a lesser extent) her *Three Guineas* that inspired my efforts here. It came as somewhat of a surprise, however, that I was also drawn to the plots and characters of Woolf's magnificent novels. More especially, it was the mystic capacity of her sentences to float within consciousness and between or among centers of sentient being that entranced me. Despite the presumption of adopting such brilliant and generically distinct models, I repeatedly experienced the need to blend her essayistic and her fictional techniques into a sort of critical *bildungsroman*, but why? Some will object that narrative exigencies obscure critical clarity, just as criticism drains narration of its subtleties, indeed that such an endeavor falls between two stools (an expression I have never understood or wanted to begin to understand). Others might judge it anachronistic to address the challenges of today and tomorrow with the rhetorical paraphernalia of yesterday, but what if the style of much recent criticism seems lifeless, formulaic, or ingrown?

Perhaps the need for narrative criticism arises when multiple perspectives, contradictory convictions, more concrete approaches to interconnected cultural problems have to be broached, or the effort needs to be made to bridge a widening gap between intellectual matters that might sound arcane or specialized but that profoundly impinge on the everyday lives of ordinary people. Not autobiographical, my turn to storytelling nevertheless uses some of the techniques of personal criticism and does so to avoid abstract theoretical languages that have seemed to me and to many others exclusionary or unintelligible; common experiences within the academy, I wished to believe, might ground highly eccentric narrative details for readers with quite varied points of view, but a shared concern with women's well-being. Flaunting its artifice, narrative's specificity, I felt, could rescue us from universalizing claims (that have historically erased women), while also grappling with the psychological and material conditions of political investments; for we think with minds saturated with affections and aversions, faiths and fears, with bodies infused by pains and pleasures, habits and hurts. And many of us, who have for so many centuries been associated more with the body and with the emotions (rather than with the disembodied brain), have often realized this. Storytellers generally seek to entertain their audiences, and feminists—who have always understood the interconnections between scholarship within the academy and social movements outside it—have often used stories to narrate changes in our conceptualizations of sex, of gender, so as to make our inquiries relevant to all those confronting rapid technological and geopolitical transformations. And although these last may fill many of us with regret or anger, apathy or high anxiety, the successes of the women's movement—though partial and limited—are a good excuse for celebration.

Still, my motives here are partly selfish, for I have so often found myself perplexed by the ideas of my contemporaries, and my students have so often found themselves flummoxed by the ideas of my contemporaries that I decided it would be cowardly not to explore the issues for myself, for my students, and through scene-making replete with hesitations and qualms, yearnings and vacillations born at the expense of footnotes and judicious specificity, scrupulous reasoning and historical archiving. Quite simply put, I was wary that too scholarly or abstract a treatment would play false, would fail to convey the more intense life of an invigorated and invigorating social and intellectual phenomenon. If I have leaned rather heavily on, borrowed rather more frequently than I should have from those who wrote before, you might consider that most of the critics of the past are inheritors as well as originators, for books did and do have a way of influencing not only us, their readers, but also each other. Like the offspring of parents, books descending from books sometimes conform and confirm, sometimes differ and revolt, much as children do, though such an analogy need not summon up Laius and Oedipus at the crossroads, as it doubtlessly would in the voluminous tomes of Professor de M.

Next, to come to a second objection, I think you might reject my story as utopian, though utopias and utopian thinking have played a noble role in feminist intellectual history. Yet, you might exclaim, not all intellectual disputes can be so easily reconciled, whether between men and women or between women and women or between methodology and what Mary Daly dubbed "methodolotry." Here my motives were not altogether selfish, for were I true to my own particular encounters in academic feminism I would of course have to contend with dispiriting instances of opportunism and acrimony, dissension and rivalry, arrogance and affectation. Despite such demoralizing experiences (and how I sometimes long to name names), there runs throughout Mary Beton's comments my conviction—or is it simply a feeling?—that higher education has been good for women, that women and the feminist movement have been good for higher education. In other words, my utopianism depends not on razing an outdated building to put a new one in its place, but instead on a belief that for quite some time feminists have profited from frequently conflicting blueprints that have nevertheless eventuated in entranceways, renovations, additional wings and arcades, skylights, and decks with unforeseen views and prospects. Its design is not made by the relation of brick to mortar, but by the relation of human beings to human beings who have permeated its structures and partitions with creative force. One has only to recall the architecture of Christine de Pizan's *City of Ladies* or Charlotte Perkins Gilman's plan for kitchenless houses to realize this is hardly a contemporary phenomenon.

To take up another metaphor (and one to which Gilman would probably object), I nevertheless want to encourage you to take Sojourner Truth's urgency to heart (as Mary Beton did), to keep things going while things are stirring. And though I dread following such an injunction with a host of generalizations about the state of men and women in the world today or about the future direction of feminism, since generalizations tend somehow to bring the tedium of bygone times when there was a rule for everything and everyone, Chloe's fate and the lives of many of Mary Beton's cohorts haunt me (as they did her), qualifying the gains that have undoubtedly been made. Though women have composed music and published poems, invented scientific cures and solved mathematical puzzles, painted extraordinary canvases and built beautiful monuments, mapped unknown stars and catalogued unknown lifeforms, established athletic records and endowed libraries, we have yet to realize fully what recent opportunity, training, encouragement, and money have just now begun to offer.

In an all too typical hyperbole, Mary Beton remarked in the course of this book that Marx and Einstein, Von Neumann and Wittgenstein, Picasso and Stravinsky never had wonderfully gifted sisters. Of course you might have objected that

Marx did in fact have such a sister, that so-and-so was actually Picasso's peer. Or other names may have come to mind: does Frantz Fanon or Duke Ellington, Satyajit Ray or I. M. Pei, Nelson Mandela or Jonas Salk have a sister, you might have been prompted to inquire. Or again you may object to the elitist notion of measuring success by the yardstick of genius, a Romantic mystification of (generally masculine) transcendence that produces self-centered people exempted from the kindness and tact that make everyday life bearable. But surely we can agree that it is for the good of the world at large that half of humanity should prosper and excel at the same level as the other half. Now my belief about, say, Von Neumann's or Mandela's sister is that she lives in you, if not in me, and in many young girls who are on their way to becoming women. But she does live, for great minds are continuing presences in need of an opportunity to walk among us in the flesh, and this possibility is now finally coming within our purview.

If we are lucky enough to evade mass warfare and ecological disaster, to live another century or so and in rooms of our own; if we cultivate habits of courage and learning, integrity and good humor in ourselves and in each other, acknowledging the permeability of the walls, gates, and doors that protect but divide us; if we work, even in poverty and obscurity, looking past the bogey of what we know to be parochial interests to see human beings in relation to their rooms but also to each other and to the multitudinous environments inhabited in common, for we live in a world not our own and not ourselves; then the opportunity will come and the dormant mathematician or political visionary, scientist or composer will put on the body that was so often laid down. Drawing her life from the lives of Shakespeare's sisters—because Shakespeare has had many sisters, of many complexions, and from many different lands (not the least of whom was the inspiration of my musings here)—she will be born. As for her coming without renewed and determined resistance to forces that would curtail women's freedom, this would be impossible. But she is coming—to be born not again, but for the first time, and to dwell among us.

SUGGESTED READINGS

MY UNDERSTANDING of Virginia Woolf has been inflected by the brilliant biography by Hermione Lee and by the scholarship of many other insightful critics, especially Elizabeth Abel, Gillian Beer, Julia Briggs, Pamela Caughie, Mary Ann Caws, Louise DeSalvo, Maria DiBattista, Anne Fernald, Christine Froula, Sandra M. Gilbert, Lyndall Gordon, Carolyn Heilbrun, Mark Hussey, Bonnie Kime Scott, Jane Lilienfeld, Jane Marcus, Andrew McNeillie, James Naremore, Ellen Bayuk Rosenman, Brenda Silver, Mark Spilka, Gayatri Chakravorty Spivak, and Alex Zwerdling.

Chapter 1: The Once and Future History of Sex and Gender

Miriam Schneir and Alice S. Rossi have each compiled a good collection of historically important feminist texts. For histories of the second wave of feminism, see Ruth Rosen's *The World Split Open* and Estelle Freedman's *No Turning Back*. Eliza Haywood's "Fantomina" has been reprinted in the *Norton Anthology of Literature by Women*, second edition, edited by Sandra M. Gilbert and myself. For early second-wave criticism (on women writers and images of women), see publications by Mary Ellmann, Shu-

lamith Firestone, Tillie Olsen, Audre Lorde, Kate Millett, Eva
Figes, Patricia Meyers Spacks, Ellen Moers, Annette Kolodny,
Joanna Russ, Louise Bernikow, Judith Fetterley, Suzanne Juhasz,
Elaine Showalter, Barbara Christian, Cora Kaplan, Lillian Robinson, Shoshana Felman, Dale Spender, and Michèle Barrett as
well as such collections as *Sisterhood Is Powerful*, compiled and edited by Robin Morgan; *Woman in Sexist Society*, edited by Vivian
Gornick and Barbara K. Moran; *Images of Women in Fiction*, edited
by Susan Koppelman Cornillon; *Feminist Literary Theory*, edited
by Mary Eagleton; *Making a Difference*, edited by Gayle Greene
and Coppélia Kahn; *The New Feminist Criticism*, edited by Elaine
Showalter; and *Feminisms*, edited by Robyn R. Warhol and Diane
Price Herndl. For histories of feminist criticism in the seventies
and eighties, see Jane Gallop's *Around 1981* as well as Janet Todd's
Feminist Literary History and Ruth Robbins's *Literary Feminisms*.
Sandra Kemp and Judith Squires have edited *Feminisms*, a useful
anthology of feminist theory and criticism after 1980.

Besides Nietzsche and Irigaray, Joan Rivière, Thomas Berger,
Laura Mulvey, Annette Kuhn, and Kaja Silverman examine man
as the surveyor, woman as the surveyed. Juliet Mitchell's and Jessica Benjamin's work on debiologizing Freud was followed by
many psychoanalytic texts by feminists, some of whom looked to
the thinking of Karen Horney, Melanie Klein, and D. W. Winn-
icott. For a feminist response to AIDS, see the writings of Paula
Treichler.

On the exploitation of graduate students and adjuncts, the
evolving profession of English, and the economic deterioration
of the humanities as well as the decline of the traditional goals of
a liberal arts education, see Bill Readings's *The University in Ruins*
as well as more recent publications by Patrick Brantlinger, Michael Bérubé, Stanley Fish, Alvin Kernan, Annette Kolodny, Cary
Nelson, Robert Scholes, and Stephen Watt.

Chapter 2: "Theory" Trouble

For an understanding of the rise of so-called men's studies, see Tania Modleski's *Feminism without Women*, Alice Jardine and Paul Smith's anthology *Men in Feminism*, Judith Kegan Gardiner's collection *Masculinity Studies and Feminist Theory*, Susan Fraiman's *Cool Men and the Second Sex*, and Sally Robinson's *Marked Men* as well as the work of Michael Awkward, Joseph Boone, Michael Cadden, Stephen Heath, Susan Jeffords, and Peter Murphy. On the essentialism–social constructionist debate, see Diane Fuss's *Essentially Speaking* as well as essays by Linda Alcoff and Joan Wallace Scott. *Conflicts in Feminism*, edited by Marianne Hirsch and Evelyn Fox Keller, contains excellent analyses of these debates as well. Anne Fausto-Sterling published her view in *Myths of Gender: Biological Theories about Women and Men*, but see also her *Sexing the Body*.

Other Continental theorists could of course also be named, including Louis Althusser, Roland Barthes, Pierre Bourdieu, Gilles Deleuze, and Félix Guattari. A text influential on feminists by Derrida is *Spurs*; by Lacan, various writings on "the signification of the phallus" and the "mirror stage"; by Foucault, *The History of Sexuality*. Catherine Belsey, in *Poststructuralism*, provides a lucid defense and overview of the influence of Derrida, Lacan, and Foucault, whereas the books and essays of Diane Elam, Nancy Fraser, Jane Gallop, Mary Jacobus, Alice Jardine, Barbara Johnson, Peggy Kamuf, Nancy K. Miller, Mary Poovey, and Jacqueline Rose supply feminist responses.

Judith Butler's *Gender Trouble* and *Bodies That Matter* established her prominence in the early nineties. Adrienne Rich's "Compulsory Heterosexuality and Lesbian Existence" has been widely anthologized. Julia Kristeva's *Desire in Language*, Hélène Cixous's "The Laugh of the Medusa," Gayatri Spivak's *In Other Worlds*, Donna Haraway's *The Haraway Reader*, Martha Nussbaum's *Sex and Social Justice*, Alison M. Jaggar's edited anthology *Living with Contradictions*, Rosi Braidotti's *Nomadic Subjects*, Genevieve Lloyd's *The Man of Reason*, and Seyla Benhabib's *Situating the Self* can serve as introductions to these influential thinkers. To this list, many others could be added, such as Somer Brodribb, Christine Delphy, Michèle Le Doeuff, Jane Flax, Nancy Fraser, Nancy Hartsock, Denise Riley, Susan Okin, and Iris Young. For personal accounts of the difficulty women experienced entering the field of philosophy, see *Singing in the Fire: Stories of Women in Philosophy*, edited by Linda Martín Alcoff.

Linda Charnes's "The 2% Solution: What Harold Bloom Forgot" is in *Harold Bloom's Shakespeare*, edited by Christy Desmet and Robert Sawyer. On feminist approaches to ethics and gender, see Carol Gilligan's *In a Different Voice* and Sara Ruddick's *Maternal Thinking*. Andrea Dworkin and Catharine MacKinnon's antipornography activism was supplemented by such publications as Dworkin's *Intercourse* and MacKinnon's *Toward a Feminist Theory of the State* as well as her more recent essays on rape, abortion, prostitution, and harassment law in *Women's Lives, Men's Laws*. A critique of the antipornography feminists by Alice Echols appears in the 1984 anthology *Pleasure and Danger*, edited by Carole S. Vance. For biological work on sex differences, see Helen Fisher's *The First Sex*. Natalie Angier writes about women with AIS in *Woman: An Intimate Geography*, while many others—for example, Stephen Jay Gould and Ruth Hubbard—critique the claims of sociobiologists. On the prejudices of presumably objective biologists of sexual difference, see Thomas Laqueur's *Making Sex: Body and Gender from the Greeks to Freud*.

Chapter 3: White Like Me

Backlash by Susan Faludi was the most widely read book on this much studied phenomenon. Sherry Ortner's classic essay "Is Female to Male as Nature Is to Culture?" as well as Nancy Chodorow's influential *The Reproduction of Mothering* turned many humanities scholars in various fields toward analyses of misogyny throughout the 1980s, as did the influential work of Dorothy Dinnerstein. All the quotations of Cooper come from *The Voice of Anna Julia Cooper*, edited by Charles Lemert and Esme Bhan. On the history of African American women, see work on each individual, especially by Catherine Clinton, Nell Painter, Phyllis Rose, and Jean Fagan Yellin. Barbara Christian's often anthologized "Race for Theory," Jacqueline Jones's *Labor of Love, Labor of Sorrow*, Paula Giddings's *When and Where I Enter*, Hortense Spillers's "Mama's Baby, Papa's Maybe," Mary Helen Washington's *Invented Lives*, Hazel Carby's *Reconstructing Womanhood*, and Deborah Gray White's *Ar'n't I a Woman?* are influential and representative publications, whereas Henry Louis Gates Jr. made a lasting contribution through his recovery and editorial work. Zora Neale Hurston's "What White Publishers Won't Print" has been anthologized by Alice Walker, whose meditations on Shakespeare's sister appear in the title essay of *In Search of Our Mothers' Garden*. Two landmark feminist books in critical race studies were *This Bridge Called My Back*, edited by Cherríe Moraga and Gloria Anzaldúa, and *All the Women Are White, All the Blacks Are Men, But Some of Us Are Brave*, edited by Gloria T. Hull, Patricia Bell Scott, and Barbara Smith. Besides the scholars named in this chapter, many others—including Carol Boyce Davies, Ann Douglas, Farah Jasmine Griffin, Ann Allen Schockley, Valerie Smith, Erlene Stetson, Claudia Tate, Cheryl Wall, and Susan Willis—have written about African American literary women from the Harlem Renaissance to the present day; scholars from Trudier Harris to Sander Gilman and Wahneema Lubiano have studied medical and popular cultural images of the black woman.

Audre Lorde's *Sister Outsider*, Angela Davis's *Race, Class, and Sex*, Michele Wallace's *Black Macho and the Myth of the Superwoman*, and bell hooks's *Black Looks* are the most often excerpted and assigned texts by these influential thinkers. Joy James and T. Denean Sharpley-Whiting's *The Black Feminist Reader* contains essays by many of the contemporary scholars mentioned in this chapter, while Andrea Gabor's *Einstein's Wife* provides a full biography of Mileva Marić. On political correctness and racial privilege, see Troy Duster, "'They're Taking Over!' And Other Myths about Race on Campus," in *Higher Education under Fire*, edited by Michael Bérubé and Cary Nelson. On the burnout of African American intellectuals within the academy, see the writings of Ann duCille and Nellie McKay; on black women and the trauma of rape, see Charlotte Pierce-Baker. About the relationships between black and white women, the essays in *Female Subjects in Black and White*, edited by Elizabeth Abel, Barbara Christian, and Helene Moglen, make important contributions.

Chapter 4: Global Poetics

Many of my narrator's and students' speculations about twentieth-century literary history are based on insights originally developed with Sandra M. Gilbert during the composing of our three-volume *No Man's Land: The Place of the Woman Writer in the Twentieth Century*, although she ought not be held accountable for their eccentric presentation here. All of the literary texts discussed in the final exams appear in the *Norton Anthology of Literature by Women*. Besides those dealing with African American women's achievements, many feminist literary historians of the nineteenth and twentieth centuries have studied the works of women composing in the English language: representative are Julie Abraham, Amanda Anderson, Isobel Armstrong, Nancy Armstrong, Nina Auerbach, Nina Baym, Paula Bennett, Alison Booth, Marianne Dekoven, Elin Diamond, Wai-Chee Dimock, Laura Doan, Rachel Blau DuPlessis, Betsy Erkkila, Margaret Ezell, Joanne Feit Diehl, Margaret Ferguson, Laurie Finke, Kate Flint, Susan Stanford Friedman, Catherine Gallagher, Gayle Greene, Margaret Higonnet, Molly Hite, Margaret Homans, Myra Jehlen, Susan Lanser,

Shirley Geok-Lin Lim, Wendy Martin, Judith Newton, Alicia Ostriker, Ruth Perry, Marjorie Pryse, Janice Radway, Tey Diana Rebolledo, Margaret Reynolds, Jane Spencer, Laura Wexler, Patricia Yaeger, and Sandra Zagarell. Essays by Marianne Hirsch and Susan Suleiman are particularly insightful on the mother-writer. In a number of books, most recently *Literature after Feminism*, Rita Felski deals with the complex relationships between feminism and aesthetics. On the treatment of the body, see Susan Bordo's *Unbearable Weight* and Elizabeth Grosz's *Volatile Bodies*.

Although their views do not accord with Marta's, Nawal El Saadawi and Leila Ahmed have produced pioneering work on women and gender issues in the Middle East and Africa. A number of influential postcolonial and cultural studies scholars have criticized Euro-American scholars' fetishization of the aesthetic, appropriation of third-world artifacts, or neglect of third-world women; prominent among them are Barbara Harlow in *Resistance Literature* and Gayatri Spivak in her often anthologized essay "Can the Subaltern Speak?" and more recently in *Death of a Discipline*. See also the creative work on third-world women by Trin T. Minha-ha and Sara Suleri.

Ngũgĩ wa Thiong'o, Taban lo Liyong, and Henry Owuor-Anyumba's "On the Abolition of the English Department" can be found in the *Norton Anthology of Theory and Criticism*, edited by Vincent B. Leitch. A number of recent anthologies collect the most prominent postcolonial critics mentioned in chapter 5. Besides individual monographs, see such collections as *Feminist Postcolonial Theory: A Reader*, edited by Reina Lewis and Sara Mills; *Feminist Theory Reader: Local and Global Perspectives*, edited by Carole R. McCann and Seung-Kyung Kim; *Scattered Hegemonies*, edited by Inderpal Grewal and Caren Kaplan; *The Challenge of Local Feminisms: Women's Movements in Global Perspective*, edited by Amrita Basu; *Third-World Women and the Politics of Feminism*, edited by Chandra Talpade Mohanty, Ann Russo, and

Lourdes Torres; and *Unthinking Eurocentrism*, by Ella Shohat and Robert Stam. Useful introductions to Chicana literary studies are furnished by Norma Alarcón, Teresa McKenna, Paula M. L. Moya, Sonia Saldívar-Hull, and Marta Ester Sanchez. Important feminist approaches to Asian American literature have been published by such critics as King-kok Cheung, Elaine Kim, Sau-ling Wong, and Anne Anlin Cheng. On postcolonial poetry in English, see Jahan Ramazani, *The Hybrid Muse*.

Many postcolonial and Chicana scholars use approaches derived from cultural studies; however, a number of feminist critics have pioneered cultural studies in British and Anglo American contexts. See the individual monographs and the anthologies produced by Lauren Berlant, Cathy N. Davidson, Sarah Franklin, Amy Kaplan, Anne McClintock, Helena Michie, Tania Modleski, Lynne Pearce, Naomi Schor and Elizabeth Weed, Sherry Simon, Ann Thompson and Helen Wilcox, Suzanna Walters, and Kathleen Weiler.

Chapter 5: Institutionalization and Its Queer Discontents

Accounts by the founders of women's studies appear in *The Politics of Women's Studies*, edited by Florence Howe, whose establishment of the Feminist Press helped promote women's studies courses. Ellen Messer-Davidow analyzes the history of institutionalization in *Disciplining Feminism*, as do the many essays in *Women's Studies on Its Own*, edited by Robyn Wiegman. Also useful are the articles in a special issue of *Feminist Studies* 24, no. 2 (Summer 1998) devoted to institutionalization. Two good examples of the sort of textbook used in women's studies courses are *Women: Images and Realities*, edited by Amy Kesselman, Lily D. McNair, and Nancy Schniedewind, and *Feminist Theory: A Reader*, edited by Wendy Kolmar with Frances Bartkowsky.

The most powerful case against institutionalization has been made by Wendy Brown in "The Impossibility of Women's Studies," *differences* 9, no. 3 (Fall 1997): 79–101. Joan Wallach Scott's quoted words appeared in "Gender: A Useful Category of Historical Analysis," *Gender and the Politics of History*. Feminist approaches to the visual arts can be found in books by Linda Nochlin, Lucy Lippard, Whitney Chadwick, Griselda Pollock, and Germaine Greer.

The foremost thinker in gay studies and queer theory, Eve Kosofsky Sedgwick, made her mark with *Between Men* and *Epistemology of the Closet*, while Monique Wittig is best known for her essays in *The Straight Mind*. The speculations attributed at the exam to Carroll Smith-Rosenberg, Bonnie Zimmerman, Lillian Faderman, Martha Vicinus, Gayle Rubin, Esther Newton, Catharine Stimpson, Terry Castle, Judith Halberstam, Lee Edelman, Wayne Koestenbaum, Leo Bersani, Marjorie Garber, and David Halperin as well as Teresa de Lauretis can be found in these various authors' groundbreaking books. For eminently readable histories of lesbian and homosexual criticism, see Annamarie Jagose's *Queer Theory: An Introduction* as well as Linda Garber's *Identity Poetics: Race, Class, and the Lesbian-Feminist Roots of Queer Theory* and the scholarship of Sue-Ellen Case, Carolyn Dever, Marilyn Farwell, Sally Munt, Judith Roof, and Carole Vance. *The Lesbian and Gay Studies Reader*, edited by Henry Abelove, Michèle Aina Barale, and David M. Halperin, provides an excellent introduction to the field. A good collection of feminist critics dealing with film—from Molly Haskell to Linda Williams—is *Feminist Film Theory: A Reader*, edited by Sue Thornham. Background on some of the lesbian filmmakers mentioned can be found in Andrea Weiss's *Vampires and Violets: Lesbians in Film*. The subject of lesbians in the modernist period has been taken up by many scholars, including Shari Benstock and Karla Jay.

Drucilla Cornell's ideas about "ethical feminism" appear in *At the Heart of Freedom: Feminism, Sex, and Equality*. The quotation from Gayle Rubin appears in "Of Catamites and Kings: Reflections on Butch, Gender, and Boundaries," in *The Persistent Desire*, edited by Joan Nestle. On the transgendered and intersexed, see Joanne Meyerowitz's *How Sex Changed: A History of Transsexuality in the United States* and Jay Prosser's *Second Skins: The Body Narratives of Transsexuality* as well as the essays in *Feminist Theory and the Body*, edited by Janet Price and Margrit Shildrick. Both the performance artist Annie Sprinkle and the pro-sex advocate Susie Bright have published a number of popular books.

From Barbara Smith's *Conditions: Five* to Marilyn Frye's *The Politics of Reality*, Barbara Johnson's *The Feminist Difference*, Minnie Bruce Pratt's *The Dirt She Ate*, Biddy Martin's *Femininity Played Straight*, and Elizabeth V. Spelman's *Inessential Woman*, feminists have questioned the invisible privileges of whiteness and heterosexuality. Prominent postcolonial critics include Lisa Lowe in *Immigrant Acts* as well as *Critical Terrains*, Rey Chow in *Writing Diaspora* as well as *Primitive Passion*, and Chandra Talpade Mohanty in her often anthologized essay "Under Western Eyes" as well as *Feminism without Borders*. The quotation from Stuart Hall appears in his "Cultural Studies and Its Theoretical Legacies," which is reprinted in the *Norton Anthology of Theory and Criticism*, edited by Vincent B. Leitch.

Chapter 6: Reproduction in an Age of Mechanical Production

For useful anthologies, see *Women, Science, and Technology*, edited by Mary Wyer, Mary Barbercheck, Donna Giesman, Hatice Örün Öztürk, and Marta Wayne; *Linking Visions: Feminist Bioethics, Human Rights, and the Developing World*, edited by Rosemarie Tong, Anne Donchin, and Susan Dodds; and *Feminist Science Studies*, edited by Maralee Mayberry, Banu Subramaniam, and Lisa Weasel. The authors listed in chapter 6 represent only a sample of frequently cited feminist books: representative texts are Ruth Bleier's *Feminist Approaches to Science*, Gena Corea's *The Mother Machine*, Sandra Harding's *The Science Question in Feminism*, Valerie Hartouni's *Cultural Conceptions*, Katherine Hayles's *How We Became Post-Human*, Evelyn Fox Keller's *Reflections on Gender and Science*, Sadie Plant's *Zeroes and Ones: Digital Women and the New Technoculture*, Michelle Stanworth's *Reproductive Technologies*, Rosemarie Tong's *Feminist Approach to Bioethics*, and Elizabeth Wilson's *Neural Geographies: Feminism and the Microstructure of Cognition*.

On same-sex parenting, see Judith Stacey and Timothy J. Biblarz, "(How) Does the Sexual Orientation of Parents Matter?" *American Sociological Review* 66, no. 2 (2001): 159–83. On the gender of plants, see Dana Dudle and Meryl Altman, "Across the Language Barrier: Plant Gender and Feminist Theory," in *Removing Barriers: Women in Academic Science, Technology, Engineering, and Mathematics*, edited by Jill M. Bystydzienski and Sharon R. Bird (forthcoming). On insects and reproduction, see the early work of Alfred Kinsey as well as Sarah Blaffer Hrdy's more recent *Mother Nature: A History of Mothers, Infants, and Natural Selection*; Marlene Zuk's *Sexual Selections: What We Can and Can't Learn About Sex from Animals*; and Lynda Birke's *Feminism and the Biological Body*. Jean Baudrillard's quoted comment appears in *The Vital Illusion*. On women's science fiction and technology, see Anne Balsamo's *Technologies of the Gendered Body*. Kimberlé Crenshaw, Patricia Hill Collins, and Patricia J. Williams have published extensively on the legal implications of racism and sexism in the context of scientific technology, the family, the workplace, and health care, while Cheri Register has written on American families' adopting children from other countries. "What Abu Ghraib Taught Me," by Barbara Ehrenreich, is quoted at the party; it appeared originally in the *Los Angeles Times* Opinion section in May 2004 and is widely available on the Internet.

Many of Mary Daly's coined words appear in her *Gyn/Ecology*. Useful books on the so-called third wave of feminism are *Listen Up*, edited by Barbara Findlen, and *Manifesta*, edited by Jennifer

Baumgardner and Amy Richards. For a smart overview of feminist critics' investment in narrative, poetic, and personal modes of writing, see Ruth Salvaggio's *The Sounds of Feminist Theory*; for exemplary writers of personal feminist criticism and memoir, see Leila Ahmed, Gloria Anzaldúa, Deborah McDowell, Nancy K. Miller, and Jane Tompkins; for a stimulating collection of essays on "The Future of Criticism," see *Critical Inquiry* 30, no. 2 (Winter 2004): 324–478.

ACKNOWLEDGMENTS

CONVERSATIONS with so many friends and colleagues found their way into this book that I know I will not be able to name them all. At my home institution, my thinking was shaped by lively debates with graduate students and faculty, in particular Ferda Asya, Purnima Bose, Matt Brim, Judith Brown, Eva Cherniavsky, Andrea and Amanda Ciccarelli, Margo Crawford, Dyan Elliott, Jonathan Elmer, Tom Foster, Johanna Frank, George Hutchinson, Barbara Johnson, Ilinca Johnston, Ellen MacKay, Maurice Manning, Manuel Martinez, Alyce Miller, Susan Moke, Sarah Murphy, Eva Sanders, Linda Smith, Janet Sorenson, Naoko Sugiyama, Rod Taylor, Esther Thielan, Rebecca Wood, and Laura Yow. With respect to my assistants, Jamie Horrocks and Julie Wise, I can only marvel at their ingenuity, pertinacity, and dedication. Along with an exceptionally smart dean, Kumble Subbaswamy, and a supportive chair, Steve Watt, many students and colleagues at Indiana University—especially those who participated in my classes on modern literature and critical theory—have shaped my views on higher education and feminism; however, my characters are fictionalized composites, not to be interpreted as based in any way upon what are usually considered real people.

In phone conversations, visits at other institutions, or e-mail exchanges, many others made resonant suggestions that enriched my reading and writing, especially Paula Backscheider, Tamara Berg, Kyeong-Hee Choi, Alice Falk, William Germano, Elena Glasberg, Michael Glier, Susannah Heschel, Wendy Hesford, Susan Ingersoll, Georgette Kagan, Jonathan Kamholtz, Chip Kidd, Wendy Kolmar, John Laudun, Leslie Lewis, Vivien Pollack, Marnie McInnes, Juliette Merritt, Carolyn Mitchell, Kate Montwieler, Vivian Pollak, Yopie Prins, Marjorie Pryse, Carol Quillen, Scott Sanborn, Carolyn Shapiro-Shapin, Sara Steger, Skip Willman, Robyn Wiegman, and Yung-Hsing Wu. A number of schools were particularly hospitable to me, especially the University of Louisiana at Lafayette, the College of Saint Rose, the University of Cincinnati, DePaul University, the University of Georgia, the University of South Dakota, the University of Virginia at Wilmington, Memorial University of Newfoundland, and Washington University in Saint Louis.

Until her death, which was a grievous loss for me and for many others, Carolyn Heilbrun stayed closely connected through communications that transmitted her keen concern for all matters related to women's well-being. At the beginning of the project, Nancy K. Miller's wry sense of humor bolstered my efforts to use narrative in the service of criticism. During the academic year 2001–2, when I participated in Princeton University's Center for Human Values, Judith Butler and Toni Morrison, Joyce Carol Oates and Nell Painter, Valerie Smith and Niza Yanay served as role models and guides. For a month in the spring of 2004, a Bogliasco Foundation Fellowship at the Liguria Study Center for the Arts and Humanities gave me the time to reflect on the issues at hand in a beautiful setting; the hospitality of Anna Maria Quaiat, Ivana Folle, and Alan Rowlin made my stay productive and happy. During too infrequent but always illuminating visits, my cousins Bernard and Colin David (as well as their families) encouraged me to think about what does and does not translate into transatlantic idioms. As for my favorite little playmates—Cassandra Miller and her brother, Benedict, as well as the indomitable Jack Lyons—they have been a source of endless delight.

Certain friends—Shehira Davezac, Mary Favret, Sandra Gilbert, Julie and Susannah Gray, Ken Gros Louis, Jon Lawrence, John Lyons, Ken and Teddy Johnston, Andrew H. Miller, Jan Sorby, Jayne Spencer, Mary Jo Weaver—may recognize confidences encoded here that will (I hope) elicit pleasure rather than pain. Mary Jo, staunch ally and cherished interlocutor, has served as a source of inspiration before and during the composition of this book in our daily phone conversations. My dear mother, Luise David, would want it to be known that she is of course in her right mind, indeed in a much more lucid state of consciousness than her daughter will ever be. With Donald Gray and with Kieran Setiya, I am grateful for intelligence so lucid and compassionate that it takes my breath away. As for Don, he continues to provide the north and south, east and west of my being; I only hope my befuddlement in too many conversations to count will be chalked up to my weird absorption in the writing process. From my daughters, who also give my existence ground and direction, I ask forgiveness too for lapses in attention: Marah and Simone embody a future I never thought possible to project into the world, and I am so very proud of them both, different though they are, for they remain (as they know) my heart's desire.

In a work as experimental as this one, I often felt doubtful or deluded, but several generous and smart readers served as steady sources of support in a way that made it possible for me to preserve faith in a composing process that always felt quirky and risky: Todd Avery, Linda Charnes, Mary Favret, Susan Fraiman, Judith Kegan Gardiner, Marah Gubar, Jamie Horrocks, Andrew H. Miller, Kieran Setiya, and Alison Umminger provided expertise in matters related to the coherence of theme, character, tone, and plot; the evolution of feminist thinking; and the quotidian realities of academic life. During my earliest and thus most frayed stages of drafting, two people—Elizabeth Abel and Tricia Lootens—never wavered in their willingness to respond with integrity, hard questions, but also loving kindness. Without their extraordinary encouragement, the project would have remained an eccentric fantasy. Needless to say, none of these readers can be held accountable for the views expressed in this book; however, all of them contributed to the pleasure I took in its composition. The sort of work they undertook is generally invisible in the academy, but this volume would not exist without their valiant acts of attention, for which I am deeply grateful.

Because the last stages of authoring can be so frustrating—when, despite all the revising, what seems a highly vulnerable package has to be stamped and mailed to the fraught world of publishing houses—I am particularly grateful for the enthusiasm and alacrity of my editor at the University of Illinois Press, Joan Catapano, as well as the insightful readers she chose. The seriousness with which she and they devoted them-selves to even minute phrasings honed not only the style but also the content of the prose presented here, as did the scru-pulous copy editing of Carol Bolton Betts. Attentive to the his-torical as well as the aesthetic repercussions of her decisions, Cope Cumpston ingeniously used her design to enhance the final publication. Jessica Gonzalez, Miriam Moore, and Bahia Quinlan provided the handwritten portions of the text.

Of course my greatest debt is to Virginia Woolf, whose sen-tences in the novels and letters, diaries and essays did what she wanted them to do, tore at the shingles at the bottom of this reader's soul, moved me over and over again through waves of anger and pain, hilarity and delight. At the beginning of the appended recommended reading list, I have listed the crit-ics who best helped me understand the resonance of Woolf's achievement in books that provide an endless source of inspi-ration for those of us whose lives and languages are made pos-sible by hers.

SUSAN GUBAR, Distinguished Professor of English at
Indiana University, is the co-author with Sandra M. Gilbert
of *The Madwoman in the Attic: The Woman Writer and the
Nineteenth-Century Literary Imagination* and its three-
volume sequel, *No Man's Land: The Place of the Woman
Writer in the Twentieth Century.* Besides co-editing the
Norton Anthology of Literature by Women, she has published
a number of books including *Racechanges: White Skin,
Black Face in American Culture; Critical Condition:
Feminism at the Turn of the Century;* and *Poetry after
Auschwitz.* In 2005 Professor Gubar provided
an introduction and notes for the first
annotated edition of Virginia Woolf's
A Room of One's Own to appear
in the United States.

❄

The University of Illinois Press
is a founding member of the
Association of American University Presses.

The design of *Rooms of Our Own* is based on the
Hogarth Press 1929 edition of *A Room of One's Own*.
It is typeset in 11.5 / 14.5 Filosofia, a contemporary
redesign of Bodoni letterforms, designed for
Emigre Fonts by Zuzana Licko in 1996.
Display type is Filosofia Unicase.
Sans serif "text messaging" was typeset
in Triplex, also designed by Zuzana Licko.
The text was typeset by Jim Proefrock
at the University of Illinois Press.
The book was designed by
Copenhaver Cumpston.
Manufactured by Sheridan Books, Inc.

UNIVERSITY OF ILLINOIS PRESS
1325 South Oak Street   Champaign, IL 61820-6903
WWW.PRESS.UILLINOIS.EDU